Journal of Biblical Literature
Monograph Series, Volume VII

TORAH IN THE MESSIANIC AGE AND/OR THE AGE TO COME

by

W. D. Davies

Professor of Biblical Theology
Duke University

SOCIETY OF BIBLICAL LITERATURE
224 North Fifteenth Street
Philadelphia 2, Pennsylvania
1952

TORAH IN THE MESSIANIC AGE
AND/OR THE AGE TO COME

Printed in the United States of America
on acid-free paper

∞

TABLE OF CONTENTS

FOREWORD

The editors of the Journal
of Biblical Literature wish to express their thanks to the Research
Council of Duke University for a
grant to defray the expense of lithoprinting this monograph by Professor
Davies,which is,we feel,a genuine con-
tribution to the study of some of the
Jewish sources of early Christian Messianic speculation. We are also grateful to Professor Alexander Guttmann of
Hebrew Union College for serving as a
reader of the manuscript.

Ralph Marcus

Editor of the Monograph Series

PREFACE

This monograph is the enlarged version of a paper read, at different stages of its composition, to the London Society for the Study of Religions, The Lightfoot Society of the University of Durham, England, and The Society of Biblical Literature at New York. It arose out of an effort to understand the interaction between Judaism and Christianity in the first century.

I am grateful to Professor Ralph Marcus for his courtesy in reading and correcting the typescript; to Professor A. Guttmann of Hebrew Union College, Cincinatti, one of the consultants for the S. B. L., for suggestions, all of which are noted in the text; and to the Research Council of Duke University for making possible the early publication of the work. I desire also to acknowledge the help of Mrs. S. R. Garren in typing my manuscript, and of Miss Joyce G. Lockhart who prepared the typescript for lithoprinting with a meticulous care. Were it not pretentious to do so, I should dedicate these pages to those friends across the Atlantic with whom I have discussed their contents --

Κοινὰ τὰ φίλων.

W. D. Davies

Duke University,
Durham, N. C.
1952.

- v -

SOURCES

The Apocrypha and Pseudepigrapha, ed. R. H. Charles, Oxford, 1931.

The Babylonian Talmud, (the customary pagination is followed); English translation, ed. I. Epstein, Soncino Press, London, 1935.

Biblia Hebraica, ed. R. Kittel, Stuttgart, 1925.

The Jerusalem Talmud, ed. Krotoschin, 1866.

Midrash Rabbah, Wilno, 1923; Warsaw; English translation, ed. H. Freedman and M. Simon, Soncino Press, London, 1939.

Midrash Tehillim, ed. Salomon Buber; German translation by A. Wünsche, Trier, Mayer, 1892-1893.

The Mishnah; English translation by H. Danby, Oxford, 1933.

Pesiqta de Rab Kahana, ed. Salomon Buber, Lyk, 1868; German translation by A. Wünsche, Leipzig, 1885.

Pesiqta Rabbati, ed. M. Friedmann, Vienna, 1880.

Philo, The Loeb Edition and Translation, 1929ff.

The Septuagint, ed. H. B. Swete, Cambridge, 1891, 1894; ed.[3] Alfred Rahlfs, Stuttgart, 1949.

Sifre debe Rab, ed. M. Friedmann, Wien, 1864.

The Targums: The Targum of Isaiah, ed. and translated by J. F. Stenning, Oxford, 1949.

The Tosefta, ed. M. S. Zuckermandel, Pasewalk, 1880.

Yalqut.

ABBREVIATIONS

E. T.   The Expository Times, Edinburgh.

H. T. R.   The Harvard Theological Review, Cambridge, Mass.

J. Q. R.   The Jewish Quarterly Review, Philadelphia.

J. T. S.   The Journal of Theological Studies, Oxford.

Other abbreviations are self explanatory.

TORAH IN THE MESSIANIC AGE AND/OR THE AGE TO COME[1]

I

INTRODUCTION

The issue raised by the non-observance of the Torah among
Gentile Christians in the primitive Church was so central that
the relation between the Torah and the Gospel could not but have
commanded much attention among historians of primitive Christianity. What is surprising, however, is that one pivotal aspect
of this relation has been little discussed. Early Christians
believed that Jesus of Nazareth was the Messiah of Jewish expectations, and that they were living in that Age which had long
been promised by the Hebrew Scriptures. It would, therefore,
seem natural that in trying to understand the interactions between the Torah and the Gospel scholars should have asked the
question what role, if any, the Torah was expected to assume in
the Messianic Age or in the Age to Come:[1] it could be assumed
that this would illumine for us the impact of the Gospel on the
Torah and thus best enlighten us on the various attitudes within
the Early Church towards Judaism and also within Judaism towards
the Church. At the same time we might expect it to lead to a
better appreciation of certain relevant elements in the Christian

---

[1]The relation of the Messianic Age to the Age to Come need
not, for the moment, concern us. In this treatise, except in
the last sections where the distinction becomes important, both
terms will be used to signify generally the ideal future of Jewish expectation. See Chapter II in J. Klausner, Die Messianischen Vorstellungen des Jüdischen Volkes im Zeitalter der Tannaiten (1904).

movement itself, as we shall hope to indicate, very briefly, at
the close of this paper.

Nevertheless, obvious and important as is its necessity,
those who have sought to clarify the role expected of the Torah
in the Messianic Age, as was suggested, have been few: the following references to the problem are the only ones we have been
able to trace. Edersheim published an appendix to his work, The
Life and Times of Jesus the Messiah (1901), Vol. II, Appendix
xiv, pp. 764ff., entitled The Law in Messianic Times: in this he
also refers to Holdheim, Das Ceremonialgesetz im Messias-Reich.[2]
Klausner dealt with the same problem in his book Die Messianischen Vorstellungen des Jüdischen Volkes im Zeitalter der Tannaiten[3] (1904), pp. 52f; in addition Kohler alloted a paragraph
to it in his article on Eschatology in the Jewish Encyclopedia,
Vol. V., p. 216, a paragraph to which Abrahams referred with ap-
proval in his Studies in Pharisaism and the Gospels, Second Series (1924), pp. 125ff. The most recent and thorough treatments
are those of Strack-Billerbeck, (Exkurse IV, pp. 1ff. Zur Berg-
predigt Jesu) (1928), and Aptowitzer in Parteipolitik der Has-
monaerzeit im Rabbinischen und Pseudepigraphischen Schrifttum,
Vienna (1927). Baeck has some interesting remarks on the question in his book, The Pharisees (E. T. 1947), pp. 72ff., and

---

[2]Not dated.

[3]A Hebrew translation, a little augmented, appeared in
Jerusalem in 1927; it is being translated into English by
W. F. Stinespring, from the third Hebrew edition, 1950.

there are scattered references in Montefiore and Loewe, A Rabbinic Anthology (1938), pp. 157ff., 558, and in the works of

Moore and Bonsirven.

The material which has been written is not bulky as evi-
dent.[4] But it has already revealed the especial difficulties

---

[4]Before we proceed to discuss it, it will not be irrelevant
to ask why this question has not attracted more attention. Apart
from the comparative ignorance of Rabbinic Judaism among Christians in general, the first answer probably lies in an insuffi-
cient understanding of the nature of apocalyptic thinking. Too
often it has been assumed that Apocalyptic was the outcome of a
mere escapism, and it was often possible to dismiss it with the
condescension, if not contempt, with which moderns usually dismiss the more bizarre forms of the Second Advent Hope. In view
of this, allied to the sharp distinction which was usually drawn
between the sober Pharisee and the fiery, day-dreaming Apocalyp-
tist, it was not recognized that Apocalyptic was the outcome of
a profound ethical seriousness, which was usually no less concerned with the observance of the Torah than was Pharisaism, and that
the Messianic hope was relevant for ethics. Fortunately we have
now been recalled to the ethical ground of apocalyptic thinking
(see A. N. Wilder, Eschatology and Ethics in the Teaching of
Jesus, pp. 30f.; H. H. Rowley, The Relevance of Apocalyptic, pp.
162), and the climate is therefore congenial to a more favourable
approach to the relation of Messianism or Apocalyptic to the
Torah.
     The second answer, possibly, is to be sought in that too
marked antithesis which it has long been customary to draw in
the Old Testament between the Law and the Prophets. Modern
critics have been dominated by the view that the Law was infe-
rior to the Prophets, or, as. H. H. Rowley has recently described
it, "that the Prophets were the advocates of a purely spiritual
religion that had no use for the sacrificial cultus, while the
creators of the Law were reactionaries who triumphed over the
teaching of the Prophets, and fastened the yoke of ceremonial
observances firmly upon the Jews." (Bulletin of the John Rylands
Library, Vol. 29, No. 2, p. 327.) This attitude has, perhaps
unconsciously, been carried over into the study of the New Testament, and it has been customary, and consequently easy, to
show that Jesus is best understood in the light of the prophetic
tradition, as the fulfilment of the prophets' hope, while, at
the same time, he has often been represented as the opponent of
the legalistic tradition in all its forms; thus, for example, a

which the sources present. These are chiefly two. First there

---

recent exponent of the intention of Jesus has isolated the prophetic tradition as that which is most relevant for the understanding of Jesus. (See J. W. Bowman, The Intention of Jesus
[1945], pp. 63ff; also C. H. Dodd in Mysterium Christi [ed.
A. E. J. Rawlinson], pp. 60f. It should, however, be noted that
J. W. Bowman also finds it possible to apply the term Torah to
Christ Himself, op. cit.) As long as this attitude prevailed,
despite the express words particularly of Matthew 5, 17-20, and
many other passages, it is unlikely that justice should be done
to Jesus as the fulfilment of the Torah as well as of Prophecy:
and it is this attitude which possibly accounts for the fact
that, while the prophetic antecedents and characteristics of
Jesus have been amply recognized, the possibility that he was
consciously fulfilling the expectation of a Messianic Torah, as
surely as He fulfilled other elements in the Messianic expectation, has not been the object of sufficient interest.
      It is still the dominant view that there is a sharp cleav-
age between the Law and the Prophets, but that it is not the only possible view has been shown convincingly by H. H. Rowley (in
the article to which we have already referred). He reminds us
that there were prophetic groups within the cultus, that within
the prophetic canon the priestly attitude is given expression,
that it was not the cultus as such that the prophets condemned
but its misuse, and that while there was undoubtedly a difference
of emphasis between Prophets and Priests there was no fundamental conflict. This reconciling tendency in Old Testament studies has a bearing upon the study of the New Testament. It prompts
the question whether Law and Prophecy, if they are not sharply
opposed in the Old Testament, are not both fulfilled in the New
Testament. Certain it is that if, as I think we should, we follow H. H. Rowley in a new evaluation of the legal portions of
the Old Testament, we should also be more prepared to set Jesus
not so much in iconoclastic opposition to the Torah as in critical fulfilment of it, and hence more anxious to enquire as to
the role ascribed to it in the Messianic Age. (See especially,
A. R. Johnson, The Cultic Prophet In Israel [1944]; for references, p. 62.)
      In the third place, it is possible that the theological
atmosphere within which New Testament, like other Biblical studies, were pursued until recently has had much to do with the
neglect of the problem with which we are concerned. That interpretation of the teaching of Jesus which saw in it an ethic that
was meant to be applied directly in this world by the aid of the
Holy Spirit tended to produce, quite naturally, an impatience
with the patient minutiae of legalism in all its forms. "To
love God and do what one liked" - phrases such as these expressed
an attitude which made it difficult to appreciate that there
might be any relevance for Christianity in the legal tradition

is the dating of the various relevant passages. Thus most of

---

of Judaism: and it was phrases such as these that what we shall
call, (for want of a better term,) Liberal Christianity employed
to describe the ethical life "in Christ"; and it is not surprising that it very often dismissed the casuistry of legalism as
mere pettifogging - a pettifoggery that was swept away by Christ.
(It is relevant to point out here that some recent scholars,
e.g. T. W. Manson, The Teaching of Jesus², p. 48, and R. Bult-
mann have increasingly recognized Rabbinical elements in Jesus'
teaching, see Jesus and the Word [Eng. Trans.], pp. 55f; K. H.
Regenstorf, Theol. Wörterbuch [hrsg. G. Kittel], Bd. ii, pp.
155ff.)
     But the temper of the theological scene has changed, not
only has life in this 'time of the breaking of the nations' so-
bered us, but the increasing recognition in recent scholarship
of the eschatological character of the teaching of Jesus and of
the absolute nature of His ethical demand has also made acute
the problem of its application of life in this world. This in
turn has made it impossible for us to be wholly contemptuous of
the so-called 'casuistry' of legalism. We now have painfully to
confess, as T. W. Manson has expressed it, "that it is much easier to denounce the scribal system than to do without it." (The
Teaching of Jesus², p. 296. The whole chapter on Religion and
Morals in this book brings the problem we are discussing to a
focus: we are however inclined to doubt Manson's too sharp distinction between the moral teaching of Jesus (at least as it
came to be understood in the early Church) and that of the
Scribes.) "The relevance of an impossible ethic" (see e.g., R.
Niebuhr, An Interpretation of Christian Ethics [1936]) - it is
phrases such as this that are now in the air, and they are in-
dicative of our dilemma. But it was this very dilemma, in a
less agonizing but no less real form, which gave birth to Jewish
legalism. That legalism was the mint of prophecy: essentially
its intention was to make relevant the prophetic ethic. Hence
it should be easier for us now to do justice to that 'casuistry'
which has too often been the object of our contempt. It may not
be a new 'casuistry' that modern Christendom needs, but it does
need to make relevant to its life an ethic that is eschatological,
and may therefore learn from that development of the Law which
attempted to meet a similar need. (Cf., e.g., E. Robertson in
Law and Religion, [ed. E. I. J. Rosenthal,] [1938], pp. 74f;
L. Finkelstein, The Pharisees [1940]). We have mentioned above
those factors in the contemporary theological situation which
should make it possible, and necessary, for us to appreciate
more fully the significance of the Torah for the Christian dispensation, and with this end in view we shall be concerned in
the above pages to discover what part, if any, the expectation
of a New Torah in the Messianic Age or in the Age to Come had in
the eschatological speculation of Jewry in the first century. In

the Rabbinic material used is post-Christian and often reveals a marked tendentiousness: and it is the weakness of Edersheim's treatment of our problem, as that of Aptowitzer,[5] for example, that they ignore the complications caused by these factors. The second difficulty arises from the precise interpretation of the Hebrew terms used in certain contexts: to note only one example, even the term Torah itself in different places may mean different things and is thus a constant source of confusion. This difficulty is brought out in Klausner's treatment of our theme and in that of Aptowitzer. Both these difficulties will occupy us later, we mention them here merely to indicate beforehand the complexity of our task: thus warned we can proceed to our examination of the sources, beginning with the Old Testament: and it should be noted at the outset that we shall be particularly concerned to discover whether or not Judaism contemplated a New Torah in the future.

But before we go on to examine the relevant texts we point out, by way of background, a highly pertinent fact suggested by the first of the passages with which we shall deal, i.e.,

---

our endeavour we shall draw upon the material used by the scholars named above, but we shall try to assess it for ourselves.

[5]v. Aptowitzer, op. cit., pp. 116ff, held that it was the politico-religious rivalries of the Hasmonaean period that stimulated speculation on the role of the Torah in the future - whether in the Messianic Age or the Age to Come. The hands of the Hasmonaeans were stained with blood so that many of the pious objected to their High Priesthood: the Pharisees also objected to their Kingship because they were not of the stock of David to whom (according to Scripture and tradition) the Kingship right-

Jer. 31$^{31-4}$, namely, the marked significance of the Exodus and
of Moses not only in Israel's history but also in its Messianic
expectation. This was not merely homiletic,[6] but also theological,

---

fully belonged. Out of this situation between Hasmonaeans and
anti-Hasmonaeans there arose disputes over the perpetuity of the
Law and its role in the Messianic Age and in the Age to Come.
The radical anti-Hasmonaeanists proposed the view that in the
future the Messiah would be of the stock of David and also High
Priest; there would be a Messiah-Priest: while the Hasmonaean-
ists looked for a Priest-Messiah; but the views of both sides
were only made possible by the manipulation of Scripture. The
Pharisaic expectation of a Davidic High Priest in particular implied that the copies of the Torah in the Messianic Age would
have to be changed, at least in parts. This in turn raised the
question of the perpetuity of the Torah. Within the Pharisaic
party Aptowitzer found a struggle. The rigourists maintained
that the Law was perpetually unchanged and unchangeable: others
held that in the Messianic Age it would be modified and in the
Age to Come abrogated; thus if the Messianic Age can be identified with the Age to Come it also would see the abrogation of
Torah. This discussion within Pharisaism was possible because
of differences over the question of the incidence of the Resurrection: did it occur at the close of the Messianic Age, then
that Age could still have its Torah; did it occur at the beginning of the Messianic Age then clearly the conditions would ap-
proximate those of the Age to Come when the Torah would be abrogated. Were there no Resurrection of all then the eternal validity of the Torah could be held, and this was the position of
the Sadducees. According to Aptowitzer this explains why the
Sadducean-Hasmonaean author of the Book of Jubilees is so insistent on the perpetuity of the Law: his insistence is not aimed at
the antinomianism of Paul, as Singer had argued, but at his political opponents. Nevertheless much of the Christology of the
New Testament in Matthew, Luke (the genealogies), Paul and He-
brews is to be understood in the light of the speculations to
which the political struggle indicated gave rise. The value of
Aptowitzer's treatment lies in the wealth of material which he
commands, not in the interpretation he puts upon it. It is precarious to use Rabbinic texts of a far later period to illumine
the struggles of the Hasmonaean period: in the words of J. Bonsirven "ces divinations sont trop conjectural pour qu'il soit
prudent d'en fait état?" (Le Judaïsme Palestinien, Vol. I,
p. 47; cp. A. Marmorstein, Monatschrift für Geschichte und
Wissenschaft des Judentums [1929], pp. 224-250; 440f; 478-487.

[6]Cf. S. A. Cook, The 'Truth' of the Bible, ad loc.

in that the first redemption from Egypt became the prototype of the future redemption.[7] Thus although Jeremiah contrasts the New Covenant with that ratified at the Exodus, nevertheless, it was that same Exodus which, were it only by contrast, supplied him with the very categories with which to describe the new redemption that he desired.[8] More striking still is the parallelism between the first and last redemption drawn in Deutero-Isaiah, passages from which we will discuss below; the last is described in terms, enhanced indeed, but, nevertheless, derived from the first. Long a common-place, this has recently been forcefully presented by Kissane. To Isaiah (42^{13} - 44^{23}) he has given the title 'The New Exodus'. The thought is that Yahweh who created Israel and redeemed her from Egypt is about to intervene once more on her behalf (42^{23} - 43^2); just as His special relation to Israel led Him to deliver her in the past, so will it involve His delivering her again in the future (43^{3-8}); the Old Exodus thus becomes the guarantee of the New (43^{9-12}),[9] when Babylon will suffer as formerly did Pharaoh (43^{14-17}) in an Exodus far more glorious than the old (43^{18-21}). The full extent

----

[7]P. Volz, Eschatologie der jüdischen Gemeinde, p. 113.

[8]There is a New Exodus doctrine in Jer. 16^{14-15}, and J. Bright, J.B.L., Vol. LXX, p. 22, is right in finding germs of it in Hosea 2^{14-15}.

[9]A. Bentzen finds here essentially the contrast later drawn between The Two Ages, Messias, Moses redivivus, Menschensohn, p. 56, "Dieser deuterojesajanische Gedanke vom 'Neuen' hat-das sei nur kurz angedeutet-in der neutestamentlichen Eschatologie seine Entsprechung. Es sei nur erinnert an 2 Korinther 5, 17b und Apoc. Joh. 21.5. Deuterojesaja arbeitet faktisch mit

to which Deutero-Isaiah is impregnated with the motif of the
Exodus can only be appreciated by a detailed study of E. J.
Kissane's treatment.[10]

Further just as the Exodus in Deutero-Isaiah is connected
with creation,[11] the Scandinavian scholars in a similar fashion,
have found in the Servant poems,[12] which, as we shall see, speak
of a Torah, both the lineaments of a New Moses and the traces of
a creation-mythology. E. Sellin[13] long since identified the Servant with Moses, and, although his reasons for doing so were
faulty, this identification was, according to Bentzen, essentially sound. Criticizing Engnell's overemphasis on the king-motif
in the Servant poems, Bentzen finds the prototype of the Servant
in Moses; especially is it true that the Servant is the New Moses,
in Isaiah 49$^{5-6, 8-12}$, and also in the passages depicting the
vicarious suffering of the Servant which Bentzen thinks are best

---

dem Gegensatz zwischen den beiden Aeonen den wir aus dem Spät-
judentum so wohl kennen." C. R. North in Studies in Old Testament Prophecy (ed. H. H. Rowley), Edinburgh, 1950, denies this,
pp. 111ff.

[10]The Book of Isaiah, Vol. 11, pp. 39ff.

[11]C. R. North, The Old Testament Interpretation of History,
pp. 48ff.

[12]For our reason for treating the Servant in a messianic
context see below, p. 29ff.

[13]For a summary of Sellin's position see C. R. North, The
Suffering Servant in Deutero-Isaiah, ad loc.; A. Bentzen, op.
cit., p. 64; H. Riesenfeld, Jesu Transfigure (1948), pp. 81ff;
H. Chavasse, Theology, Vol. LIV, August, 1951, pp. 295f, follows
E. Sellin.

understood in the light of verses such as Exodus 32[31ff], Deut.
9[17-20, 25-29], and again Deut. 1[37], 3[26], 4[21].[14]

We need not be committed to his interpretation to recognize the significance of Bentzen's insistence on the concept of
the New Moses for the understanding of the Servant poems: at
least it is entirely consonant with what we have previously
found in Deutero-Isaiah. Moreover, the importance of Moses in
eschatological thinking is abundantly clear from other sources.
The evidence for this is presented by Volz[15]: "the Prophet" who,
in accordance with Deut. 18[15], was expected to appear in the future was often identified with Moses both in the Apocrypha and
Pseudepigrapha, among the Samaritans, and in the Rabbinical docu-
ments. The Age to Come came to be regarded as a return to two
previous periods which might be regarded as "ideal," namely, the
period of the sojourn in Paradise, and that when Moses lived,
and the principle came to be established that the last Redeemer
would correspond to the first. The marks of the Mosaic period
would find their counterpart in the Age to Come.[16]

---

[14]Op. cit., p. 65.

[15]Op. cit., pp. 194ff: for the Moses redivivus among the
Samaritans see P. Volz, op. cit., (summarising M. Gaster) p. 62.
But see also for Deut. 18[15] in Rabbinic sources below pp. 52, 87,
and 89, n. 8.

[16]For the significance of Moses in the mind of Israel see
Johs. Pedersen, Israel, III-IV, pp. 54ff. This persisted in
Hellenistic Judaism. See e.g. Philo, On the Life of Moses, Book
I: Philo's desire is ἀναγράψαι τὸν βίον ἀνδρὸς τὰ πάντα
μεγίστου καὶ τελειοτάτου.
Later we meet the colossus in the murals at Dura-Europos: See M.
Rostovtzeff, Dura-Europos and its Art, Oxford, 1938, p. 111. Ac-
cording to M. Rostovtzeff Moses is here almost deified: he is a

So familiar is this correspondence between the Mosaic and
the Messianic periods that we need not enlarge upon it. For our
purpose Volz's presentation of the evidence suffices,[17] because
it is only one possible element in this correspondence that particularly concerns us. We are especially concerned to discover
whether Messianic speculation made the attempt to carry this correspondence to its logical conclusion and thus came to demand a
Messianic Torah as a counterpart to the Mosaic Torah. North has
claimed that "There is nothing in the prophets to indicate that
the covenant was concluded at Sinai in particular, as distinct
from the Exodus proper. This is not to say that the prophets
were ignorant of the Sinai tradition," but North only hesitating-
ly adds, "though it may well be that Galling (Die Erwählungs-
traditionen Israels [Giessen, 1928], pp. 26-37) is right in his
surmise that for their religious consciousness the act of deliverance, the Exodus itself, was the immediate occasion of the covenant relation between Yahweh and Israel, rather than any deliverance of specific laws at Sinai."[18] But Galling's position we

---

counterpart to Christ. His importance for the Rabbis cannot, of
course, be exaggerated. See below p. 89, n. 8.

[17]Op. cit., pp. 195ff, 359ff, 113f. See also H. J. Schoeps,
Theologie und Geschichte des Judenchristentums, Tübingen (1949),
pp. 87ff, for much relevant material and references. Also H.
Riesenfeld, op. cit., index on Moses. On the whole subject of
Moses in Palestinian and Hellenistic Judaism see J. Jeremias,
Theologisches Wörterbuch, Bd. IV, pp. 852ff.

[18]Op. cit., pp. 52f.

find difficult to accept. Surely it is false to separate the
covenant relation from what North calls the "deliverance of specific laws." The element of demand was integral to any covenantal relationship, and it would seem safer to regard the Exodus in
such covenantal connections as generally including, implicitly
at least for the prophets, the whole complex of events at Egypt,
the Red Sea, and Sinai. North's hesitancy in fully endorsing
Galling's position is therefore justified. This hesitancy would
also seem to be confirmed by what we shall find below concerning
Deutero-Isaiah and the Suffering Servant.[19] The new redemption
was to be like the first, and we shall see that in agreement with
this the Servant was to have his Torah.   Mt. Sinai also figures
in later Messianic speculation; again we refer to Volz[20] for the
evidence, and although what he presents bespeaks nothing specifically of a new or Messianic Torah, it is well to remember that
we pursue our specific quest into the Old Testament and other
sources against a very rich complex of concepts such as the New
Covenant, and the New Exodus to which we have here referred, a
complex which might perhaps be expected to contain at least in-
cipiently the concept of a New Torah. The relevant passages are
the following.

[19]See below p. 29ff.
[20]Op. cit., p. 360.

II

IN THE OLD TESTAMENT

The ground has been prepared for us in this matter by G. Östborn, in his book <u>Tōrā in the Old Testament</u> (Lund, 1945). There are passages which reveal clearly that in the ideal future, however conceived, the imparting of תֹּורָה, whatever its exact significance, would be a function of the Deity Himself or of His agent. We shall examine the passages in what would seem to be that chronological order which is most generally adopted.

(A) <u>Jeremiah 31</u>[31-4]

This is the most crucial, perhaps, of the passages with which we have to deal (though it is also the most tantalizing). Even its authenticity has been denied and its significance consequently deemed to be trivial, if not banal. Thus Duhm[1] placed the passage in the Maccabean period. We need not enlarge upon his reasons, stylistic and other, for taking this position: here we are only concerned to recall that he strongly denied that the passage possessed that spiritual depth which Christian scholarship has usually read into it. To Duhm the verses merely pointed to the desire for a new covenant after the pattern of those previous covenants which had marked the Exodus and other events in Israel's history. This becomes clear from the fact that no new kind of Torah is mentioned in the passage, but merely a new cove-

---

[1]B. Duhm, <u>Israels Propheten</u>[2] (1922), pp. 456f.

14

nant, formulated, it is implied, on the basis of the existing
Torah. Under the new covenant contemplated, it is the demands
of the old Torah, both moral and ceremonial, that are to be obeyed; and what the author desiderates is that every Israelite
should know those demands by heart, without the necessity of any
human teacher's insistent instruction. This was also the ideal
of the Deuteronomist, who has often, and wrongly, been compared
unfavourably with Jeremiah. Hence we should not regard these
verses as introducing new conceptions of the nature of the covenant between Yahweh and His people; indeed, Duhm argued that
there was no reason why, if the form of the old Torah was unsat-
isfactory, Yahweh should have introduced Israel to that particular form at all; surely, were it necessary, He would and could
already at the Exodus have introduced the better form, which, it
is claimed by Duhm's critics, is desiderated in these verses.

The glaring lack of historic perspective displayed in
this last judgement of Duhm's need not detain us,[2] and the whole
position he maintained has often been severely criticized,[3] and

---

[2]See J. Skinner, Prophecy and Religion, ad loc.

[3]C. Cornill in particular argued against B. Duhm in Einleitung in Das A.T. (1913). The following accept the authenticity of the passage: J. A. Bewer, The Literature of the Old Testament in its historical development (New York, 1922), p. 165; J.
E. Binns, The Book of the Prophet Jeremiah, Westminster Commentaries (1919), pp. 241ff; A. Condamin, Le livre de Jeremie
(Paris, 1920), p. 237; S. R. Driver, The Book of the Prophet
Jeremiah (1906), p. 1; F. Giesebrecht in Handkommentar zum A.T.
(ed. W. Nowack), 1907, ad loc; G. B. Gray, A critical introduction to the Old Testament, (1913), p. 196; W. F. Lofthouse,
Jeremiah and the New Covenant (1925); F. Nötscher, Das Buch

although some later scholars[2] have followed Duhm in regarding it
as post-Jeremianic, the consensus of scholarship is in favour of
accepting the authenticity of the passages concerned; and in the
light of this consensus we must now examine its contents: it
reads as follows:

> 31 Behold, the days come, saith the Lord, that I will
> make a new covenant with the house of Israel, and
> with the house of Judah: not according to the cove-
> nant that I made with their fathers in the day that I
> took them by the hand to bring them out of the land of
> Egypt; which my covenant they broke, although I was an
> husband unto them, saith the Lord. 33 But this is the
> covenant that I will make with the house of Israel af-
> ter those days, saith the Lord; I will put my law in
> their inward parts, and in their heart I will write
> it; and I will be their God, and they shall be my
> people: 34 and they shall teach no more every man his

Jeremias (Bonn, 1934), pp. 234f; W. O. E. Oesterley and T. H.
Robinson, An Introduction to the Books of the Old Testament
(1934), pp. 304, 309; A. S. Peake, Jeremiah, Century Bible (1929),
p. 248; H. H. Rowley, The Growth of the Old Testament (1950), p.
102; Hans Schmidt, Die Schriften des Alten Testaments, Zweite
Abteilung (1923), p. 372; E. Sellin, Introduction to the Old
Testament (Eng. trans., W. Montgomery, 1923), p. 150; J. Skinner,
op. cit., ad loc.; G. A. Smith, Jeremiah, Baird Lecture (1922),
pp. 375ff; P. Volz, Der Prophet Jeremia (in Kommentar zum A.T.),
Leipzig, 1922, pp. xlvi, 279f; A. C. Welch, Jeremiah: His time
and his work (Oxford, 1928), (but he confesses to a certain
sympathy with B. Duhm) pp. 229f.

[4]These are chiefly O. Eissfeldt, Einleitung in das Alte
Testament (1934), p. 407 (but he admits that the thought of the
New Covenant is consonant with that of Jeremiah); A. Bentzen also seems to favour classifying this passage with those revealing
a background of later times and markedly Deutero-Isaianic dic-
tion, Introduction to the Old Testament (1949), pp. 117f; G.
Hölscher (so W. O. E. Oesterley and T. H. Robinson, op. cit.,
pp. 304 n.i.); S. Mowinckel, Prophecy and Tradition, ad loc. Two
recent books I have not been able to consult, H. Rudolph's commentary (Tübingen, 1947), and H. Ortmann, Der alte and der Neue
Bund bei Jeremia (Berlin, 1940).

neighbour, and every man his brother, saying, Know
the Lord: for they shall all know me, from the least
of them unto the greatest of them, saith the Lord;
for I will forgive their iniquity, and their sin
will I remember no more. (A.V.)

The significant factors are the following. For Jeremiah the relation between Yahweh and His people in "the days to come" will
be covenantal: the covenant which will then come into being will
be a new one: one element in it, as in all covenants, will be
Torah. But, whereas in previous covenants the Torah involved
was written on some outward material, and, in the particular
covenant which Jeremiah had in mind, written on tablets of stone,
in the new covenant the Torah will be written "in the heart," or
"in the inward parts"; and whereas the writing of the previous
Torah was accomplished by human means, the Torah in the new covenant will be inscribed by Yahweh Himself. Moreover the Torah in
the new covenant will not need to be taught by human teachers,
because all who participate in the new covenant will "know" the
Lord; and they will share in this knowledge because the barrier
to it, sin, has been forgiven by God. As a result of all this
Israel will become the people of Yahweh and He their God.

Our main concern is with the Torah which Yahweh will
write in the 'inward parts,' or 'in the hearts' of His people.
G. A. Smith[5] insisted that here, as so often elsewhere, the term
תּוֹרָה should be interpreted not as 'Law' in the sense of legal
codes, but as instruction or revelation. Moreover, in view of

---

[5]op. cit., p. 377.

the immediacy of Yahweh's activity in putting His Torah in the
'inward parts' and in writing it 'in the hearts' of the members
of the New Covenant, and also in view of the emphasis on the
knowledge of Yahweh, which it would involve in the future envisaged by the prophet, most Christian scholars have concluded
that Jeremiah here introduces a new conception of that covenantal
relation between 'Israel' and Yahweh which would ultimately prevail, a new conception which in effect nullifies the necessity
of all Torah in any external sense. A. S. Peake's expression of
this position will suffice as typical. "The New Covenant is new
not in the sense that it introduces a new moral and religious
code, but that it confers a new and inward power of fulfilling
the code already given. The law ceases to be a standard external to the individual, it has become an integral part of his per-
sonality."[6] And again, "The law written on the heart implies an
inner principle which can deal with each case of conscience sym-
pathetically as it arises, and can ensure the fulfillment of its
behests, because it has brought the inner life into perfect har-
mony with itself. The heart, and thus the whole life, has with
the engraving of the law upon it, itself become new. The heart
embraces not only the emotional and ethical but also the intel-
lectual life. And thus, by being transformed from a foreign ru-
ler into a native and inward impulse, the law gains the power of
self fulfillment.[7] In agreement with this is G. Quell in the

---

[6]Jeremiah, The Century Bible, Vol. II, p. 103.
[7]Ibid., p. 106.

Theologisches Wörterbuch zum Neuen Testament. To him the New
Covenant is really no Covenant, the law in the heart no law. The
categories of 'covenant' and 'law' have been transcended.[8]

In confirmation of the above, it has been claimed that the
yearning for a covenant new in kind, in which there would apparently be no external Torah, is illuminated for us, and, therefore, reinforced in its historical probability, by the circum-
stances of Jeremiah's life. It was his poignant experience of
the failure of the Deuteronomic reform movement that led Jeremiah
to question the efficacy of the outward forms of religion and
their necessity, and so created in him a distrust of written
Torah in all its forms.[9] Östborn[10] has conveniently summarized
much of the recent discussion on this point. He refers to Volz's
view that "in the time of Jeremiah, Israel's leaders were inves-
tigating the _possibility_ of fulfilling the divine commands" (our
italic); this, so Volz suggests, was because the people had so
resisted the demands of the prophets: and it was this same re-
sistance that compelled Jeremiah to speak of a new kind of covenant. Volz argues that Jer. 7[7ff] seems "to warrant the inference

---

[8]Band II, p. 126f.

[9]See T. H. Robinson, A _History of Israel_, Vol. 1, p. 429;
H. H. Rowley, _Studies in Old Testament Prophecy_ (1950), pp. 157ff.

[10]_Op. cit._, pp. 152ff. Johs. Pedersen who is doubtful of
the authenticity of the passage, takes it to demand "a psychic
transformation," "an intense change of disposition, a conversion,"
see _Israel_, III-IV, p. 566. Cf. P. Volz, _Der Prophet Jeremia_,
p. 293ff, who thinks that Jeremiah wishes to see the earth
peopled by godlike people.

that in the prophet's opinion the very circumstance that "the
law" has been recorded in writing has come to thwart the reali-
zation of "the law" in agreement with those ideas the prophet
expresses in Jer. 31[31-4]." Similar to Volz's position, according to Östborn, is that of G. von Rad.[11]

If the scholars mentioned above are to be followed, then
the concept of an outward Torah is really transcended and even
annulled in the New Covenant envisaged by Jeremiah. There are
certain considerations, however, which incline us to suspect this
view as, at least, an overstatement. Let us begin with the last
point made, namely, that Jeremiah was in sharp reaction against
Deuteronomy. Östborn[12] points out that von Rad, although agree-
ing in the main with Volz, nevertheless departs from him in
claiming that none of Jeremiah's words suggest that he had rejected Deuteronomy. This was the position long since reached by
Skinner. "In spite of differences," he writes, "there are close
affinities between the school of Deuteronomy and the teaching of
Jeremiah. The mere fact that the prophecies of Jeremiah were
edited by the Deuteronomic school shows that there was no consciousness of antagonism between them. Deuteronomy as well as
Jeremiah insists on the need of a circumcision of the heart (Jer.
4, 4; Deut. 10, 16; 30, 6); and the author of the principal

---

[11]In Das Gottesvolk im Deuteronomium (Stuttgart, 1929), in
Beiträge zur Wissenschaft vom Alten und Neuen Testament.

[12]Op. cit., p. 154.

edition of Deuteronomy .... inculcated so earnestly the inward-
ness of true obedience as springing from love to God, that we
can almost think of him as a disciple of the prophet, or a Me-
lanchthon to his Luther. Moreover the steadfast loyalty of the
family of Shaphan till the end of Jeremiah's life suggests that
he never broke openly with the reforming party, and certainly
makes it extremely improbable that he had denounced them as a
clique of forgers and deceivers."[13] This is not to deny that
Jeremiah was of a different spirit possibly to the Deuterono-
mists: but that difference can be grossly exaggerated. Recently
this point of view has been maintained with much emphasis by
Rowley.[14] He makes it clear that we can overemphasize the distrust of the written Torah, as of other outward forms of religion,
in Jeremiah's mind. The prophet was probably not so much discon-
tented with the written Torah as such, as with the Torah which
was merely written in a book or on tablets of stone or any other
outward material: he could express discontent with the written
Torah without wishing to imply that it was necessarily evil in

---

[13]Op. cit., ad loc.

[14]Op. cit., p. 345. See, however, A. Bentzen, op. cit.,
pp. 118ff, where he speaks of the process of 'deuteronomizing'
that has gone into the reporting of Jeremiah's work (so also B.
Duhm and S. Mowinckel). A. Bentzen speaks of the 'radicalism'
of Jeremiah "breaking through the orthodox varnish," especially
in his polemic against the cultus. This implies that H. H. Rowley's position does not sufficiently recognize the way in which
Jeremiah's radicalism has been modified by deuteronomistic re-
vision. Nevertheless H. H. Rowley has historical probability on
his side and A. Bentzen does not meet J. Skinner's treatment of
the theme.

itself, and, therefore, had to be transcended.

From this we go on to point out that it was possible to speak of the written Torah as being 'in the heart'. This means that the express terms used by Jeremiah in connection with Torah in the New Covenant do not necessarily exclude some form of written Torah. Östborn[15] indeed refers to several passages - Deut. 17^{19}; Josh. 1^8; Ps. 1^2, 37^{31}, 40^8 - as containing the concept of the Law being written in the heart or in the inward parts. But of these only two are strictly permissible, namely, Ps. 37^{31}, 40^8. The former reads:

> The Law of his God is in his heart
> None of his steps shall slide.

This passage is dated by C. A. Briggs[16] in the period of Nehemiah when the Torah was beginning to assume its subsequent dominance over Israel's life. W. F. Cobb[17] regarded Psalm 37 in its entirety as Messianic: it is those who now have the Law in their heart who will enjoy the Messianic blessings in the future. Psalm 40^8 reads:

> I delight to do thy will, O my God:
> Yea, thy Law is within my heart.

---

[15] Op. cit., p. 151, n. 1.

[16] I. C. C., Psalms, Vol. 1, ad loc.

[17] The Book of Psalms (1905), ad loc.

Cobb[18] here found a reference to Jer. 31[31ff], and it is possible that it is the influence of Jeremiah that accounts for the concept expressed, and the same applies to Psalm 37[31]. It might, therefore, at first sight appear as though we should not use these passages to corroborate our interpretation of Jeremiah, because they themselves may be the product of Jeremiah's own influence. But this is not the case. If the passages were produced under the impact of Jeremiah, they merely prove that Jeremiah's thought of a New Covenant could be reconciled with the thought of a <u>written</u> Torah and was, in fact, interpreted in that light by his successors.

Moreover, there are other passages to be noted, especially Deuteronomy 30[14]; the whole passage reads:

> For this commandment which I command thee this day, it <u>is</u> not hidden from thee, neither <u>is</u> it far off. 12 It <u>is</u> not in heaven, that thou shouldest say, Who shall go up for us, to heaven, and bring it unto us, that we may hear it and do it? 13 Neither <u>is</u> it beyond the sea, that thou shouldest say, Who shall go over the sea for us, and bring it unto us, that we may hear it and do it? 14 But the word <u>is</u> very nigh unto thee, in thy mouth, <u>and in thy heart</u>, that thou mayest do it. (A. V.)

The thought of verse 14 is also expressed in Deuteronomy 6[7] and 11[19]. In all these passages the Torah, i.e., the written code of laws, can be regarded as having been so much impressed upon "Israel" that it can be said to be upon or in their hearts.

---

[18]<u>Op</u>. <u>cit</u>., <u>ad loc</u>.

It is possible that our position can also be reinforced by another consideration. In the elucidation of Jer. 31[31ff], Östborn,[19] like others before him, refers to Ezekiel 11[9] and 36[26ff]. Without attempting to justify his procedure, he uses these passages to introduce the idea that it is Yahweh's spirit which teaches Torah in the New Covenant.[20] Now, if it be permissible to use Ezekiel in this manner, and if the passages referred to in Jeremiah and Ezekiel are 'messianic,'[21] then it will also follow that the Torah of the New Covenant will be the old Torah. This is made clear in Ezekiel 36[27f], where the 'new heart' and the 'new spirit' are expressly connected with the written statutes and judgements of Yahweh.

It follows from all the above that the reference in Jeremiah 31[31ff] to a Law written 'in the heart' or 'in the inward parts' does not necessarily imply any rejection of the written Law as such. In a confused manner Östborn has recognized this, but insufficiently; he merely concedes in a footnote that: "To judge from our previous findings, Torah 'in the heart,' 'in the inner man,' would appear to allude to the consciousness of Yahweh's 'will' ('Law') felt by a man in whom the 'Spirit of Yahweh

---

[19]Johs. Pedersen, Israel, III-IV, p. 581, calls the keeping of the Torah in the heart a fundamental idea of Deuteronomy.

[20]Op. cit., p. 151. See Paul and Rabbinic Judaism, p. 224.

[21]The term is here used in a general sense as referring to the ideal future.

resides. However, this need not imply any opposition - not on principle, at least - to the written "Law."[22]

But before we draw our conclusions we have, finally, to meet G. A. Smith's contention that Torah in Jer. 31[31ff] should be translated by instruction or revelation in a general sense.[23] We must insist over against this that the context, that of a covenant, here seems to demand a translation which will somehow preserve for תּוֹרָה its connotation as the element of demand (both ethical and ceremonial) in the covenant, i.e., the part played by Law. The Targum does not help us at this point; it translates תּוֹרָתִי by אוֹרָיְתִי , which is ambiguous, like תּוֹרָה itself. But the LXX seems to corroborate our view. One manuscript translates תּוֹרָתִי by νόμον which is the obvious translation: but the majority of MSS have νόμους ; and this, as the reading of B., was followed by Swete: it may be that it is used by the LXX so as to make it clear what the reference is - it is to the many demands of the Torah.[24] To all this

---

[22]Op. cit., p. 155, n. 3.

[23]Op. cit., p. 377.

[24]See S. H. Blank in Hebrew Union College Annual, Vol. vii (1930), The Septuagint Renderings of Old Testament Terms for Law, p. 278f. In view of his treatment, the use of νόμους for תרתי hardly seems accidental. There seems to be no reading תורתי which could have underlain it. Where תורה is rendered by terms other than νόμος those terms are often in the plural. Here in Jer. 31[33] only in B. and a scribal correction to א do we find the plural νόμους for תורה (sing). The plural νόμους for sing. תורה is very rare. Blank only refers, in addition, to B. to 2K.14[6]; A. to Jer. 26[4], a marginal

G. A. Smith[25] has in effect replied that in expressing new conceptions Jeremiah, like all others, had to use old words: point-
ing out that the term 'covenant' was not "unnatural to Jeremiah
nor irrelevant to his experience and teaching"; that its associations as he had recalled them had been those "not of law but of
love," he claimed that covenant was only a metaphor to describe
a relation which was really beyond the compass of any figure;
and how else than by those terms that he used, asked Smith,
"could the prophet have described an inward and purely spiritual
force?"[26] We cannot dissent from the view that the term "cove-

---

correction in Q. to Jer. 44[10] and א to Prov. 28[7]. Usually
even a plural תורות in the M. T. was rendered by νόμος
(sing.). This difficulty of the text at Jer. 31[33] is not mentioned by A. W. Streane, The double text of Jeremiah (Cambridge,
1896), p. 218f, nor by P. Volz, Studien zum Text des Jeremia
(Leipzig, 1920), p. 237f. G. C. Workman, The Text of Jeremiah,
(Edinburgh, 1889), ad loc., notes that the LXX translates
תורתי while the Massoretic text has תורתי : but this
may be due, he suggests, to the fact that the vowel letters י
and ו were used very variably and often omitted. "Had these
letters," he writes, "been always written in the translators'
MS where they are now written in the Hebrew text many significant
deviations could not have occurred." He mentions 49 cases in
Jeremiah where the ו was omitted and 32 where the י was omitted. If G. C. Workman is correct, we have in Jer. 31[33] another
instance of the LXX translator being confused by the omitted ו .
See R. R. Ottley, A Handbook to the Septuagint, p. 113. (Com-
pare S. R. Driver, Hebrew Tenses, p. xiii to which he refers.).
In this case the LXX has no theological bias in rendering תורתי
of the M. T. by νόμους . On the other hand, S. H. Blank's
study must be given full consideration and we have allowed for
it in our treatment, i.e. νόμους (pl.) for תורתי (sing.)
is intended to make clear that it is the many demands of the
Torah that Jeremiah has in mind.

[25]Op. cit., ad loc.

[26]Op. cit., ad loc.

nant" came naturally to Jeremiah's lips: we may also admit that
there is a fleshly screen in all language. But Smith's contrast
of law and love, would be alien to Jeremiah's thought. The
giving of the Law was in itself, we cannot sufficiently emphasize, a mark of Yahweh's love, and at this point Smith is surely
reading back into the Old Testament a false antithesis derived
from later Christian theology.

We are now in a position to seek to assess the passage in
Jer. 31 anew. It is possible to argue that the covenant envisaged by Jeremiah in the future would be a new covenant demanding
a new kind of Torah apparently of a kind which may best perhaps
be called 'pneumatic' in the sense that it involved the activity
of an inner, spontaneous principle. At the same time, however,
we have seen reason to question that sharp antithesis to the old
written Torah which this has been claimed to imply. We have had
to recognize a certain tension in his thought between the written Torah and the Torah to be dispensed in the "new covenant,"
and we have been unable to resolve this tension into a complete
difference. It is Östborn and Skinner, who have perhaps best
recognized this tension in Jeremiah's thinking, in which the old
and the new stand in uneasy juxta-position. Östborn,[27] as we
saw, must be included among those for whom there is a Torah of a
new kind involved in the New Covenant but a Torah which is called such only for want of a more adequate term. But he is uneasy

---

[27]Ibid.

about this interpretation. He is at pains to insist that the Torah in the heart need not imply any opposition in principle to the written Law and thus recognizes that it was possible to be conversant with "the same religious and ethical ideas as characterize the inner, pneumatic Torah" and yet accept the book of the Law.[28] Skinner also reveals the same uneasiness: he is constrained to admit that the New Covenant involved a new Torah: for him the essence of the prophecy lies in the "spiritual illumination of the individual mind and conscience, and the doing of the will of God from a spontaneous impulse of the renewed heart," and so the "Tora of Yahweh is the living principle of religion which is ever new, which exists perfectly in the mind of God, and is therefore capable of being reproduced in the minds of men who 'know Yahweh' in spirit and in truth." But Skinner is also careful to insist that in the written Torah also the essential will of God had been at least partly expressed.[29] Both Östborn and Skinner are struggling to preserve in their concept of the new Torah that duality which marks Jeremiah's thought of the Torah, as of nationalism, the desire to preserve and yet to fulfil. What we are concerned to emphasize is that Torah, new in some sense and yet not divorced utterly from the old Torah, i.e., an external Torah, is part of Jeremiah's hope for "the latter days." For Jeremiah the New Covenant would probably demand both the letter and the Spirit.

---

[28]Ibid.

[29]Op. cit., ad loc.

*Page number 27 omitted in error.

(B) The Servant of Yahweh and Torah

We now come to passages later than Jeremiah; we have already referred to some verses in the Psalms where it may be that we are to trace the prophet's influence: these we shall not need to discuss further; and we proceed to the Servant passages in Deutero-Isaiah.[30] The reason why we turn to these is that while, as North[31] has recently concluded, it is not possible to prove that the Servant was originally conceived as the Messiah, nevertheless, that figure is highly pertinent in any discussion of Old Testament Messianism. From New Testament to modern times there has been a constant stream of Messianic interpretations of the Servant;[32] and recently this has been reinforced by the

---

[30]Snaith, Studies in Old Testament Prophecy (Essays presented to T. H. Robinson), pp. 188ff, argues against the separation of the Servant-Passages from the rest of Deutero-Isaiah. The consensus of scholarship is against him.

[31]The Suffering-Servant of Deutero-Isaiah, ad loc.

[32]In the Targum of Jonathan, ben Uzziel, the Talmud, the Fathers, the Reformation: and since J. C. Döderleim's work in 1771 up to B. Duhm, the majority of scholars both Catholic and Protestant; all these witness to the possibly Messianic character of the Servant. Since B. Duhm the Messianic interpretation has found support from both Protestant and Roman Catholic scholars, namely, Julius Ley, L. Laue, G. Füllkrug (though he speaks of the Servant as a soteriological rather than as a Messianic figure), A. van der Flier, A. Mäcklenburg, E. Ziemer, H. Gressmann, J. Schelhaas, A. H. Edelkoort, O. Procksch among Protestants; and F. Feldmann, A. Condamin, A. van Hoonacker, J. Fischer, J. S. van der Ploeg, among Roman Catholics. (For bibliographical details see C. R. North, op. cit., whom we have followed.)

Scandinavian School. I. Engnell,[33] H. S. Nyberg,[34] A. Bentzen
have all, in different but related ways, interpreted the Suffering Servant as the Messiah. A most convenient discussion is
that of Bentzen, _Messias_, _Moses redivivus_, _Menschensohn_ (Zürich,
1948), where, beginning with the now familiar interpretation of
many Psalms as cultic material connected with the Jewish New Year
Festival when the drama of creation was re-enacted, he proceeds
to show how the figure of the king in these Psalms is Messianic,
but is also to be identified with the _Urmensch_ and, finally,
with the Suffering Servant, and the Son of Man, all figures which
were originally elements in a great cosmic myth whose pattern is
traceable all over the Ancient East.[35]

There is, therefore, impressive support for the Messianic
interpretation of the Servant. But, as North's survey shows,
there are also other interpretations with massive support. Nevertheless, even if the direct Messianic interpretation of the
Servant be rejected and the mythological one be not convincing,
as most British scholars seem to judge,[36] we have further to

---

[33]See _The Bulletin of the John Rylands Library_, Vol. 31,
No. 1 (1948).

[34]A summary of his position is given by C. R. North, _op.
cit._, _ad loc._

[35]For criticism of the Scandinavian position, see N. H.
Snaith, _The Jewish New Year Festival_ (1948); A. R. Johnson,
_E. T._, Nov., 1950, p. 39, n. 7, rejects N. H. Snaith's position.

[36]C. R. North, _op. cit._

consider William Manson's[37] suggestion that in the pre-Christian era the figure of the Servant came to be closely related to, if not actually merged or identified with, the Son of Man and the Messiah. Rowley[38] strongly dissents from any such identification, but it is favourably received by Black[39] (apparently) and by J. Jeremias.[40] We need only refer to our discussion of this elsewhere.[41] In any case, however, whether the identification in pre-Christian times be accepted or not, the Messianic significance given to the Servant by, most probably, Christ[42] and certainly by His Church makes the consideration of the relation of the Servant to Torah necessary here.

And from our point of view it is highly significant that many scholars have been led to see in the Servant a teacher of the Law, this especially on the basis of the first of the Servant poems, Is. 42^{1-4}. North renders it as follows:

---

[37]Jesus the Messiah, pp. 171ff.

[38]The Relevance of Apocalyptic, p. 57; The Biblical Doctrine of Election, and fully in, Oudtestamentische Studiën, Deel viii, ed. by P. A. H. de Boer, ad loc., where the relevant literature is surveyed; cf. T. W. Manson, J. T. S., April, 1950.

[39]E. T., October, 1948.

[40]Nuntius, Uppsala, Vol. 1, No. 1; see H. H. Rowley, op. cit., for other references.

[41]Paul and Rabbinic Judaism, pp. 279ff.

[42]Contrast e.g., C. T. Craig, The Journal of Religion, Chicago, Vol. XXIX, 1944, pp. 240-245.

```
1    Behold!  My Servant whom I uphold,
     My chosen in whom I delight!
     I have endowed him with my spirit,
2    He shall announce judgement ( מִשְׁפָּט ) to the nations
     He shall not cry nor make any clamour,
     Nor let his voice be heard in the street;
3    A reed that is bruised he shall not break,
     And the wick that burns dimly he shall not quench.
     Faithfully shall he announce judgement,
4    Not burning dimly nor himself being bruised,
     Until he have established judgement in the earth,
     And for his instruction ( תּוֹרָתוֹ ) the far coasts
          wait eagerly.
```

The first scholar to emphasize the Servant as a <u>Toralehrer</u> was Duhm.[43] Emphasizing that the term מִשְׁפָּט in 42^2 is a kind of summary term for the total "law" of Israel, he regards the mission of the Servant as the giving of the "law," which Israel already had, to the other nations.[44] In this interpretation of מִשְׁפָּט he has been followed by Skinner[45] who defines it to mean "the religion of Jehovah regarded as a system of practical ordinances"; and by G. W. Wade[46] who writes of it as "a collective expression for the divine requirements both ceremonial (2 Kings 17^{26-7}) and moral (Jer. 5^4)." In this he is to be preferred to T. K. Cheyne[47] who quite unjustifiably confined מִשְׁפָּט here to moral demands. Duhm's interpretation of the Servant has been followed by Bertholet, details of whose position are given

---

[43]<u>Das Buch Jesaia</u> (1914), pp. 284ff.

[44]E. J. Kissane, <u>op</u>. <u>cit</u>., Vol. II, p. 36.

[45]<u>Cambridge Bible for Schools, Isaiah XL-LXVI</u>, p. 27 (1911).

[46]<u>The Book of the Prophet Isaiah, Westminster Commentaries</u>, <u>ad loc</u>.

[47]<u>The Prophecies of Isaiah</u>, Vol. 1 (1884), <u>ad loc</u>.

by North.[48] For his own part North[49] also discusses whether the Servant gives his מִשְׁפָּט as a travelling preacher or as a king: he comes to the conclusion that "the phrase suggests decisions uttered by someone vested with executive authority. His authority may be exercised mildly - "A bruised reed he shall not break'[50] - but the implication is that he could be severe if he wished." On the other hand, the impartation of Torah suggests that the Servant is also a prophetic figure. Östborn[51] would see in the Torah of the Servant a mark of his kingship, but he seems to do violence to the evidence when he makes the king in Israel too much the imparter of Torah; the passages he quotes show that the king was expected to maintain Torah but not necessarily that he mediated Torah.[52] The fairest conclusion seems

---

[48]Op. cit., p. 49.

[49]Op. cit., pp. 141f.

[50]R. Marcus in H. T. R., Vol. XXX, No. 4, Oct. 1937, pp. 249ff, translates Isaiah 42³ freely as follows: "A crushed reed he may be, but one that no one shall break; a dimly burning wick he may be, but no one shall quench its light; in spite of everything he shall bring justice to the nations." Like C. R. North and N. H. Snaith he sees severity in the Servant. He takes תּוֹרָתוֹ to mean 'teaching': and מִשְׁפָּט "the suppression of immorality and idolatry and so salvation for mankind" (p. 251).

[51]Op. cit., pp. 56ff.

[52]This problem has again come to the fore through I. Engnell's insistence on the character of the Servant as King. The term ʿebed he regards as originally a royal cultic title (Bulletin of John Rylands Library, Vol. 31, No. 1, p. 69, n. 4). This concept he applies to all the Servant passages. On Isaiah 42¹ff he writes that "it looks most like an oracular assertion in which the royal qualifications of the Servant are accumulated:

34

to be that the Servant is both a kingly and prophetic figure; and in view of his kingly character, Skinner's[53] comment is apposite that the best commentary on Is. 42^{1-4} is Is. 2^{1-4}, which shall occupy us next. Before we go to this we repeat that the imparting of Torah is a central function of the Servant of Yahweh: this Torah will be directed to the world. It may not be possible, on the basis of their probable subsequent identification, to ascribe the same function directly to the Messiah but in any case, the function of the ideal Servant - be he people, individual, Messiah or other, is to impart מִשְׁפָּט and תּוֹרָה.

(C) Isaiah 2^{1-5} (with parallel, offering from our point of view only unimportant variation, in Micah 4^{1-5}).

---

he is upheld, chosen, beloved, possessing the spirit; he also has his own תּוֹרָה or מִשְׁפָּט , his royal judicial function, the discharging and extending of which is his special task." He refers in comparison to J. Begrich, and E. Burrows, who defines מִשְׁפָּט as "the right of the Messianic House of David, as in Ezekiel." Similarly in Isaiah 49^2 I. Engnell refers the words "and he made my mouth like a sharp sword," not to the prophetic art of speaking but to the royal pronouncement of judgements. Again 50^{4-5} depicts the Servant as a diviner, "which tallies with the fact that the King was in principle the only oracle receiver...." (Ibid., p. 71.) And 50^{10} is translated, "Whosoever of you feareth Yahweh should listen to the voice of His Servant, who walketh in darkness having no light, but trusteth in the name of Yahweh and stayeth upon his God." A. Bentzen has joined issue with I. Engnell in all this, even though he recognizes the mythological background for the Servant passages that I. Engnell assumes. It is as a prophet that the Servant is conceived in 42^{1ff}; in 49^{1-13} he regards the Servant as a New Moses: in 50^{4-5} the Servant has been to the school of his Divine Lord. So too A. Bentzen urges that in 52^{13}, 53^{12} the author has a contemporary prophet or even himself in view. (See Bulletin of Rylands Library, ibid.; A. Bentzen, op. cit., pp. 46ff.)

[53] Isaiah XL-LXVI, p. 27.

The word that Isaiah the Son of Amos said concerning
Judah and Jerusalem. 2 And it shall come to pass in
the last days that the mountain of the Lord's house
shall be established in the top of the mountains,
and shall be exalted above the hills; and all nations shall flow unto it. 3 And many people shall go
and say, Come ye and let us go up to the mountain of
the Lord, to the house of the God of Jacob; and he
will teach us of his ways, and we will walk in his
paths, for out of Zion shall go forth the law
and the word of the Lord from Jerusalem. 4 And he
shall judge among the nations.... (A. V.)

The phrase בְּאַחֲרִית הַיָּמִים , "in the end of the

days," is ambiguous. S. R. Driver defines it as "the final

period of the future so far as it falls within the range of the

speaker's perspective."[54] It is, therefore, not strictly Mes-

sianic and is not regarded as such by Wade.[55] Other scholars,

the vast majority, however, take it so in this context; we men-

tion Cheyne, Driver, Duhm, Gray, Peake. In any case the passage

clearly refers to that final aeon, when God's will should be

done, and in that sense we may broadly term it Messianic, even

if it has no explicit reference to the Messiah. In Messianic

times then Jerusalem is here pictured as the religious centre of

the world, whence Yahweh Himself will instruct people in His

ways. Torah shall go forth from Zion, and His word from Jeru-

salem.

But the exact significance of the term תּוֹרָה here, as

so often, is difficult to assess. The LXX renders it by νόμος

---

[54] I. C. C., Deuteronomy, p. 74.

[55] The Book of the Prophet Isaiah, Westminster Commentaries,
p. 15.

"law," but this means little because the LXX often uses $\nu\acute{o}\mu os$ for $\Pi\dot{\gamma}\dot{i}\Pi$ where we should rightly expect such words as $\delta\iota\delta\alpha\chi\acute{\eta}$, $\delta\iota\delta\alpha\sigma\kappa\alpha\lambda\acute{\iota}\alpha$ or some other derivatives of verbs used to translate $\Pi\dot{\gamma}\dot{i}\Pi$.[56] And most scholars have concluded that because of the absence of the article, the parallelism with "the word of Yahweh," and the fact that it is non-Israelites who utter the words under discussion, the term is more akin to 'instruction' in a general sense than to "law" either written or oral. It is so taken by Gray, Wade, Powis-Smith,[57] Duhm, and Östborn. But two things should be stated in this connection.

First the date of this passage has been variously assessed. Wade, Peake, Powis-Smith all point out that its ideology is post-exilic: the conversion of the nations, the pilgrimage to Zion, these are ideas typical of the post-exilic prophets. The phrase $\mbox{בְּאַחֲרִית הַיָּמִים}$ itself is first applied Messianically in Ez. 38[16]. Gray also inclines to a late date in view of all this. Duhm's view that the section was by Isaiah himself makes its position in Micah and its title in Is. 2[1], which shows that it has no connection with what preceded, sources of difficulty.[58] On the other hand, its context in Micah does not suggest

---

[56]C. H. Dodd, The Bible and the Greeks, p. 32.

[57]I. C. C., Micah, ad loc.

[58]O. Procksch, Jesaia, 1 (Leipzig, 1930), ad loc., thinks that the question of its Isaianic authorship cannot be decided. The best treatment of the thought of the passage is by E. J. Kissane, The Book of Isaiah (1941), Vol. 1, p. 26. He accepts its authenticity. Note that G. B. Gray does not take אַחֲרִית הַיָּמִים to be necessarily late in its Messianic sense, I. C. C., Isaiah, I-XXXIX, p. 44.

the authorship of that prophet, the transition from 3^9-12 being
too abrupt; and Jer. 26^18 makes the ascription of 4^1-5 to Micah
very improbable. But, although its meaning is instruction in a
general sense, if the passage is post-exilic we must beware of
emptying the term תּוֹרָה here of all reference to the Law. In
the post-exilic period it would naturally draw to itself a more
legal connotation, because the instruction of Yahweh was increasingly being thought of in terms of 'the Law' which was princi-
pally expounded at the sanctuary by prophet and priest. Indeed
the homiletic reflection found in verse 5, which unites vv. 1-4
with what follows in v. 6ff, shows that the instruction referred
to is "the light of the Lord," which, as Gray points out, refers
to the path lighted by the Law. We can be certain that the per-
sons who incorporated this poem in Isaiah and Micah, while they
might have thought of the תּוֹרָה referred to in Is. 2^3 = (Micah 4^2) as general instruction, would not in the least have regarded this as in any way incompatible with the legal tradition
in Israel. Thus Cheyne is most emphatically to be rejected when
he suggests that there is a contrast implied here between the
Jerusalem of the future and the Sinai of the past "whence the
earlier and more limited revelation proceeded." The 'instruction' of the future Jerusalem would be, we cannot doubt, in line
with the Torah of Sinai.

The second factor to be noted is that we here meet with
Yahweh Himself as a teacher, and we are possibly to think of
Him as teacher in virtue of his kingship; certainly He will

38

judge in virtue of this. Östborn[59] claims that part of Yahweh's
kingly rule in "the latter days" would be the imparting of
Torah. He cites Robertson Smith who has familiarized us with
the view that from the first the Divine King of the Israelites
had to give counsel by oracles or soothsayers in matters of national difficulty, and a sentence of Justice when a case was too
hard for ordinary decision. We have above questioned Östborn's
view; and North seems to differ from him: the latter, as we saw,
denies that the king gives Torah. Nevertheless, Östborn and
North would agree that the Servant of Yahweh can be both prophetic and kingly in Is. 42[1] (he can give מִשְׁפָּט and תּוֹרָה)
and we may also think of Yahweh Himself in the ideal future as
both exercising the kingly function of giving מִשְׁפָּט and
the 'prophetic' function of giving תּוֹרָה .

---

[59]Op. cit., p. 150.

III

THE APOCRYPHA AND PSEUDEPIGRAPHA

We have now examined the evidence of the Old Testament.
Next we shall turn to the Apocrypha and Pseudepigrapha, which
introduces us to the relevant apocalyptic literature. Ever
since R. H. Charles'[1] brilliant presentation of it, the view
has been all too easily accepted that Apocalyptic was the only
true development of the prophetic tradition, a development which
had perforce to assert its rights within Judaism, and that under
the cloak of pseudonymity, against the crippling tyranny of the
Law. Referring to the process whereby the Law came to be regarded as the final word of God to Israel, Charles wrote: "By such
drastic measures prophecy was driven forth from the bosom of
Judaism, and has never since been suffered to return. The task
of leading the people into more spiritual conceptions, alike as
regards the present life and that which is to come, devolved
henceforth on apocalyptic, and that a pseudonymous apocalyptic."[2]
But Charles' presentation of the relation between Pharisaism and
and Apocalyptic no longer satisfies. We have argued elsewhere[3]

---

[1]See Apocrypha and Pseudepigrapha (1913), Vol. II, pp.
viiff. See also F. C. Burkitt, Schweich Lectures, 1913, Jewish
and Christian Apocalypses, pp. 14ff.

[2]Op. cit., p. viii, n. 1. For a penetrating analysis of
the relation of Apocalyptic with Law and Prophecy see T. W.
Manson, Some reflections on Apocalyptic, in Aux Sources de la
Tradition Chrétienne, Mélanges offerts a M. Maurice Goguel,
Paris, 1950, pp. 139ff.

[3]E. T., Apocalyptic and Pharisaism, July, 1948; also Paul
and Rabbinic Judaism, p. 9f.

that between these two factors in the life of Jewry no great gulf was fixed, and that while there is a difference of emphasis in Apocalyptic and Pharisaic circles, nevertheless, there was no cleavage between them; and in their attitude to the Law they were at one; indeed, some of the Apocalyptists were probably as strict in their adherence to the Law as were the Pharisees themselves, and we can be fairly sure that what the former would have to say about the Law would, usually at least, command the assent of the latter.

What then does this literature reveal as to the function of the Law in the ideal future? Here again the material relevant to our purpose is scanty.[4] The following are the only passages that we have been able to glean.

(1) We first turn to I Enoch. We have to recognize that the Similitudes of Enoch, from which we draw our material, like other parts of I Enoch, have been very variously dated.[5] Here, however, we must accept the general consensus of opinion that they are pre-Christian, and thus assume that we can use them for our purpose, with full awareness, however, of the strictures of J. Y. Campbell[6] and others on those who follow this practice.

---

[4]Thus there is no passage cited by R. Marcus, Law in the Apocrypha (1927), which is immediately relevant to our purpose.

[5]See H. H. Rowley, The Relevance of Apocalyptic, pp. 52f, 75f.

[6]J. T. S., Vol. XLVIII, 1947, p. 146: it may be that the recently discovered Dead Sea Scrolls can settle the date of

In a vision, which he calls a vision of wisdom, Enoch is granted to see that which is to come. To him is revealed the coming judgement of the wicked (Chapter 38), the abode of the Elect One, who is marked by righteousness (Chapter 39); and later it is revealed to him that this Elect One or the Son of Man is very closely associated not only with righteousness but also with wisdom. Thus in 48^1 we read:

> And in that place I saw the fountain of righteousness
> Which was inexhaustible:
> And around it were many fountains of wisdom:
> And all the thirsty drank of them,
> And they were filled with wisdom,
> And their dwellings were with the righteous and holy
>   and elect.
> And at that hour the Son of Man was named
> In the presence of the Lord of Spirits,
> And his name before the Head of Days.

Further on there is mention again of the power and wisdom of the Elect One who is to be the judge of the righteous and the wicked "in those days" that are to come. Chapter 49^{1f} reads:

> For wisdom is poured out like water,
> And glory faileth not before him for evermore.
> For he is mighty in all the secrets of righteousness.

and in 51^3 we read:

> And the Elect One shall in those days sit on My throne,
> And his mouth shall pour forth all the secrets of
>   wisdom and counsel
> For the Lord of Spirits hath given (them) to him...

I Enoch, but see W. F. Albright, The Old Testament and the Archaeology of Palestine, in The Old Testament and Modern Study, ed. H. H. Rowley, Oxford, 1951.

There is in all the above, it is true, no specific reference to the Torah. But we cannot doubt that for the author of the Similitudes the righteous are those who have been faithful to the Torah and it is in accordance with the Torah, we can be sure, that the Elect One shall judge (see 38^2, 39^6, 46^2, 53^6). The association of the Elect One with wisdom may also be significant because from early times wisdom had been associated with Torah as in Deuteronomy 4^6, and as early as Ecclesiasticus was actually identified with the Torah. The passage concerned from Ecclesiasticus is interesting; it reads (24^{3ff}):

```
3    I came forth from the mouth of the Most High
     And as a mist I covered the earth....
5    Alone I compassed the circuit of heaven
     And in the depth of the abyss I walked.
6    Over the waves of the sea, and over all the earth,
     And over every people and nation I held sway.
7    With all these I sought a resting place
     And said, In whose inheritance shall I lodge?
8    Then the Creator of all things gave me commandment,
     And he that created me fixed my dwelling place
        (for me),
     And he said: Let thy dwelling place be in Jacob
     And in Israel take up thine inheritance.
```

In verse 23 the identification of Wisdom with the Torah is made explicit:

```
     All these things are the book of the Covenant
        of God Most High
     The Law which Moses commanded (as) an heritage
        for the assemblies of Jacob.
```

Here Wisdom has found the completely satisfying home in the Torah on earth. Now in I Enoch this view is not found. Instead we have a curious passage, which looks like an interpolation in

its present context, where the view is expressed that Wisdom
searched the earth in vain for a satisfactory home and failing
to find such returned to heaven. The passage (I Enoch 42^{1ff})
reads:

> Wisdom found no place where she might dwell;
> Then a dwelling place was assigned her in the
>   heavens.
> Wisdom went forth to make her dwelling among
>   the children of men
> And found no dwelling place:
> Wisdom returned to her place,
> And took her seat among the angels....

It agrees with this that there are several passages where
it is claimed that Wisdom in its fullness is the mark of the
Messianic existence, see 48^1, 49^{1f}, cf. 5^8, 91^{10}, 2 Bar. 44^{14};
Charles comments on Wisdom in 42^{1f} that "she will return in Messianic times"; and with Wisdom, we may confidently repeat, goes
the Torah in its fullness.

(2) Next we refer to the Psalms of Solomon which are generally dated in the first century B. C. In the famous Psalm
contained in chapter 17 the Messiah is endowed with wisdom and
understanding (29f, 42): he is claimed to be taught of God (34);
his word will be powerful in judgement (41); and it is implied
that his judgement will not only be powerful, but penetrating
(48). There is nothing in the context to suggest, however, that
he will bring a new Law but merely that he will establish a condition when the life of righteousness in accordance with the
Torah will prevail.[7]

---

[7]See H. E. Ryle and M. R. James, The Psalms of Solomon,
pp. 143 n. on verse 37 (in their text).

(3) There are two passages to be noted next in I Maccabees where it is made clear that it was expected that certain
difficulties which beset the interpretation of the Law in the
present would be made plain at some future date. The first
passage is in I Macc. 4⁴⁶, and reads:

> And (Judas) chose blameless priests, such as had de-
> light in the Law; and they cleansed the Holy Place,
> and bare out the stones of defilement into an unclean
> place. And they took counsel concerning the altar of
> burnt offerings, which had been profaned, what they
> should do with it. And a good idea occurred to them
> (namely) to pull it down, lest it should be a reproach
> unto them because the Gentiles had defiled it; so they
> pulled down the altar and laid down the stones until
> a prophet should come and decide (as to what should
> be done) concerning them. (μέχρι τοῦ παραγενηθῆναι
> προφήτην τοῦ ἀποκριθῆναι περὶ αὐτῶν.)

The second passage is from I Maccabees 14⁴¹:

> And the Jews and the priests were well pleased that
> Simon should be their leader and high priest for
> ever, until a faithful prophet should arise.(ἕως
> τοῦ ἀναστῆναι προφήτην πιστόν.)

In both the above passages difficulties are referred to
a coming prophet who should have a communication from God which
would solve these difficulties. The reference to a coming prophet may be based upon Deuteronomy 18¹⁵ which we know was probably
referred in the early Church to the Messiah (John 1²¹, ²⁵; 6¹⁴;
7⁴⁰; Acts 3²²ᶠ). But there is no evidence that "the prophet" in
these passages from I Maccabees should be interpreted messianically. Nevertheless, they may be cited as evidence that the
Torah would at least be better understood in the future than in
the present. Further than this we cannot go. At this point we

may best refer also to a passage in Ezra 2[63] (and parallel in Nehemiah). The unrecorded priests are here denied the right of fulfilling their priestly functions until someone - a priest - should arise qualified for this work, i.e., a priest who could use Urim and Thummim. It is clear that the use of these had been forgotten in the post-exilic community, and Kennedy contrasted the desire for a prophet in I Maccabees with the desire for a priest to use Urim and Thummim in Ezra-Nehemiah and saw in the contrast a sign of the deepening of the understanding of Israel as to the true method in which God's will was made known.[8] But this is unjustifiable, for the desire for the return of Urim and Thummim persisted. (See Tosefta, Sotah 13[2] where it is clear that it was later believed that the Messianic Age would witness their return.)

(4) Finally, it may be permissible to refer to a significant figure who appears in the so-called Zadokite or Damascus Fragment. The various dates ascribed to this work make its use for our purpose very precarious.[9] But even though the dating of the Fragment may constitute a problem, it is highly significant that a group of people should be led to constitute themselves into the people of a New Covenant, and in doing this should also be led to postulate that in the future a teacher should arise who would be able, not indeed to impart a New Torah, but to offer

---

[8] H. D. B., pp. 838ff.

[9] See H. H. Rowley, op. cit., ad loc.

additional or new interpretations of the existing Torah. This
figure is called The Teacher of Righteousness (1^7, 8^{10}, 9^{53}),
The Unique Teacher (9^{29B}, $39B$), The Teacher (9^{50}); and he is expected to arise in the end of the days (8^{10}). Until he comes
the members of the New Covenant cannot hope to know more than
they already know of the Torah, but it is expected that he will
have new things to reveal. This comes out clearly in 8^{6-10}:

> The well is the Law, and they who digged it are the
> penitents of Israel who went forth out of the land
> of Judah and sojourned in the land of Damascus, all
> of whom God called princes. For they sought Him and
> His glory was not turned back in the mouth of one
> (of them). And the Law giver is he who studies the
> Law in regard to whom Isaiah said, 'He bringeth
> forth an instrument for his work'. And the nobles
> of the people are those who came to dig the well by
> the precepts in which the Law giver ordained that
> they should walk throughout the full period of the
> wickedness. And save them they shall get nothing
> until there arises the Teacher of Righteousness in
> the end of the days.

The identity of this Teacher of Righteousness is disputed.
Charles distinguishes him from the Star who arose (9^8). The
Star he thought "does not symbolize the Messiah, but (merely)
the religious leader of the party of penitents that went to the
land of Damascus. Hence there is no connection between the idea
in our text and in Test. Lev. xviii.3; Test. Jud. xxiv.1, where
the Star does symbolize the Messiah, and where both passages are
based on Num. xxix. 17. Since the Star is said to study the Law
(דרש התורה), and likewise to have gone forth at the head
of the penitents of Damascus, he is the same as the Lawgiver in

viii. 5, 8, 9."[10] Schechter,[11] on the other hand, identified
the Star and the Teacher of Righteousness, and goes on further
to equate them with the Messiah in viii. 10 (see also ix[10B], 28B,
xv4; if viii[2] be interpreted as referring to the Messiah we have
here an interesting juxtaposition of Moses and the Messiah). The
Messiah will be none other than the Teacher of Righteousness
redivivus, and it is difficult not to agree with Schechter in
this. If he is to be followed, then the Damascus Fragment en-
visages a teaching Messiah who will reveal new truths out of the
Torah.[12]

Our survey of the Old Testament, the Apocrypha and Pseudepigrapha is now complete. When we ask what evidence it supplies for the role which the Torah would play in the Messianic
Age, we can assert that that Age was expected to be a period
when the rebelliousness of 'Israel' would be undone and righteousness enthroned, and that we have had no reason to believe
that in most, if not in all cases, this righteoueness would differ from that which was demanded by the Torah; and we may en-
dorse the words of Moore as far as the Old Testament, the

---

[10]Apocrypha and Pseudepigrapha, Vol. 11, p. 816; see also
p. 800, n. 7.

[11]Fragments of a Zadokite Work edited from Hebrew MSS,
Cambridge, 1910, p. xiii.

[12]It is unlikely in view of what we have written above that
such a conception of the Messiah could only arise among periph-
eral sects in Judaism, and G. Friedrich surely goes too far when
he implies that for Judaism the teaching of the Messiah would be
insignificant, Theologisches-Wörterbuch, Bd. 11, p. 723.

Apocrypha and Pseudepigrapha are concerned at least that "Inasmuch as the days of the Messiah are the religious as well as the political consummation of the national history, and, however idealized, belong to the world we live in, it is natural that the law should not only be in force in the Messianic Age, but should be better studied and better observed than ever before; and this was indubitably the common belief."[13] Nevertheless, we have encountered noteworthy features of the Messianic hope as it touches upon our quest. The belief was obviously cherished that the Torah would be interpreted in a more satisfactory and glorious fashion, and would also come to include the Gentiles in its sway. We failed to decide definitely whether Jeremiah's hope that there would be a new covenant implied a New Torah or whether it merely involved better obedience to the old Torah, or again whether Jeremiah expected a condition of affairs in which no external Torah of any kind would be necessary. We suggested, however, that a certain tension between the written Torah and that Torah which would mark the New Covenant was probably not resolved by Jeremiah, although those who succeeded him appear to have understood his words as still referring to the old Torah: it is clear, moreover, that the hope of a new covenant[14] persisted as a dynamic element in Judaism as is witnessed to by the Zadokite

[13]Moore, _Judaism_, Vol. 1, p. 271.

[14]See Baruch ii:35 where the covenant of the future probably looks back to the New Covenant of Jeremiah and Ezekiel. See R. Marcus, _Law in the Apocrypha_, (1927), p. 13.

<u>Fragment</u>, and it is well to remind ourselves again of the rich
complex of concepts - covenantal, Mosaic and Exodus which in-
formed the eschatological hope of Judaism.[15]

---

[15]Since the above was written, we have to take note of the
recent discoveries made in the wilderness of Judaea to which Bo
Reicke has applied the name <u>Die Ta ͑āmire-Schriften</u>. Through
the kindness of Dr. H. H. Rowley I saw an offprint of Bo Reicke's
article in <u>Studia Theologica</u> ii.i (published C. W. K. Glerrup,
Lund, 1949), entitled <u>Die Ta ͑āmire-Schriften und die Damaskus-
Fragmente. Vorschläge zur Bezeichnung der in der Wüste Juda ge-
fundenen hebräischen Handschriften nebst einigen Bemerkungen zu
diesen Texten und zu den verwandten Fragmenten der Damaskus-
Sekte</u>. The Ta amire MSS have set the problem of the date of
<u>the Damascus Fragment</u> in an entirely new light. Bo Reicke
sketches the history of the problem (p. 49f) and points out that
of the three dates that have been suggested - the Greek, Roman,
and the 7th and 8th centuries A.D., the choice really lies between the first two periods. It is here that the <u>Ta ͑āmire
Texts</u> come to our help. These are reminiscent of <u>the Damascus
Fragment</u> in their phraseology, the organisation of the communi-
ties concerned and their mode of thought. Especially significant is the fact that in the roll containing the text with 'commentary' of Habakkuk (<u>Hab. Ta ͑ām</u>) the Teacher of Righteousness,
who also figures in the <u>Damascus Fragment</u>, occurs eight times;
and there are other points of contact between the <u>Ta ͑āmire
Texts</u> and the <u>Damascus</u> Fragment (p. 53). The enemies of the <u>Ge-
meinde</u> in these new texts are the <u>Kitti'im</u> who are Hellenizers.
And in the light of all this - and other internal evidence in
the <u>Damascus Fragment</u> itself which had been previously noticed -
Bo Reicke regards it as proved that the <u>Damascus Fragment</u> be-
longs to the Greek period. He sums up his position thus: "Die
Ta ͑āmire - Gemeinde und die Damaskus-Sekte erweisen sich somit
als auf vielen Punkten mit der vormakkabäischen und der frühe-
sten makkabäischen Zeit verbunden. Die Entstehung der Texte
dürfte später liegen, aber die Entstehung der grundlegenden Be-
wegung ist allem Anschein nach in diese Zeit zu setzen. Die Ge-
meinden können aber kaum identisch sein, wegen der geograph-
ischen Verhältnisse. Die Damaskus-Sekte scheint übrigens eine
spätere Stufe zu vertreten." (p. 63.) Bo Reicke further points
out contacts between the new texts and Ezra and Nehemiah (pp.
64ff) and suggests that the teacher who is to appear "in the
end of the days" is Nehemiah <u>redivivus</u>. This last view has not
found much favour. Since Bo Reicke wrote W. H. Brownlee has
examined <u>The Jerusalem Habakkuk</u> Scroll, and compared the <u>Cove-
nanters of the Dead Sea Scrolls</u> with the <u>Covenanters of Damascus</u>
(See <u>Bulletin of American Schools of Oriental Research</u>, Dec.
1950). He agrees with M. Burrows that the Judaean Covenanters

IV

THE RABBINICAL SOURCES

When we turn to the Rabbinical sources in our attempt to
discover what role the Torah was expected to play in the Messianic Age, we must first begin by recognizing a commonplace. By
the first century that movement which received its greatest impulse from Ezra, and which was designed to make Jewry a people
of the Torah, had come to full fruition, with the result that
the Torah had become the corner stone of Jewish life. The significance of this fact can be grasped not only from Jewish history where loyalty to the Torah was the crucial factor governing
religious activity in politics and other spheres, but also from
the glorification of the Torah in Jewish thought. As Moore[1] has

---

share a common origin with the Covenanters of Damascus in the
early second-century B. C. (See M. Burrows, The Dead Sea Scrolls
of St. Mark's Monastery, New Haven, 1950.) W. H. Brownlee favours (though not without hesitation) identifying the Teacher of
Righteousness with the Messiah. (See A Comparison of the Covenanters of the Dead Sea Scrolls with three Christian Jewish
Sects, B. A. S. O. R., September, 1950. He pointed out to me a
reference in The Jerusalem Habakkuk Scroll 24 (Col. viii. L 1f)
which in the light of the N. T. insistence on faith is interesting. "The meaning concerns all the doers of the Law in the house
of Judah whom God will deliver from the house of judgement for
the sake of their labour and their faith in the Teacher of
Righteousness." The date of the Dead Sea Scrolls is still in
debate, but despite the objections of G. R. Driver, The Hebrew
Scrolls, Oxford, 1951, and S. Zeitlin, in numerous articles in
the J. Q. R., the majority of scholars in this field favour an
early dating. See in addition A. Dupont-Sommer, The Dead Sea
Scrolls, Blackwell, Oxford, 1952, English translation by M.
Rowley. According to an article in The Manchester Guardian,
April 7, 1952, p. 4, New Finds in Palestine, more recent dis-
coveries confirm the pre-Christian dating.

[1] Judaism, Vol. 1, p. 274.

made clear, so central was the Torah for Judaism that it could
conceive neither of the present nor of the past and future except
in terms of Torah. The significance of the Torah in the present
is demonstrated by that regulation of all life in its minutest
details in accordance with the Torah which ultimately led to the
codification of The Mishnah, a codification which was not a mush-
room growth but the fruit of much previous codification which
goes back at least to the first century.[2] The significance of
the Torah in the past was secured by the development of the belief that the Torah was not only pre-existent - as were certain
other pivots of Jewish life - but also, and more vitally, instru-
mental in the creation of the world. The evidence for this need
not be repeated here, because it is only with the Torah in the
future that we are concerned, and the place of the Torah in the
future was guaranteed by the development of the "doctrine" which
we know as that of the immutability of the Torah.[3]

This "doctrine" we may briefly characterize as follows.
The Torah, whether written or oral, had been given to Moses by
Yahweh. As the gift of Yahweh and as the ground plan of the Universe it could not but be perfect and unchangeable; it was impossible that it should ever be forgotten; no prophet could ever

---

[2]H. L. Strack, Introduction to the Talmud and Midrash[5],
pp. 20ff.

[3]See G. F. Moore, op. cit., Vol. 1, pp. 263ff. See also
on the above P. Volz, op. cit., especially pp. 113ff, and p. 101.

arise who would change it, and no new Moses should ever appear
to introduce another Law to replace it.[4] This was not only Palestinian belief but also that of Hellenistic-Judaism. Moore[5]
quotes Philo in a passage where he contrasts the unchanging
Torah with the ever changing laws of other nations: "The provi-
sions of this law alone, stable, unmoved, unshaken, as it were
stamped with the seal of nature itself, remain in fixity from
the day they were written until now, and for the future we expect them to abide through all time as immortal, so long as the
sun and moon and the whole heaven and the world exist." Moore
suggested that the association of the Torah with Wisdom helped
in the development of this view. We are also tempted to find,
as we shall point out later, that a certain polemic motive entered into the insistence on the "doctrine." But whatever be the
contributory factors in its rise, and it is far too pronounced
and early merely to be a polemic reaction against Christian
teaching, we can be certain that the words in Mt. 5^{18} adequately
express what came to be the dominant "doctrine" of Rabbinic Judaism.[6]

Thus the developed (Rabbinic) Judaism revealed to us in

---

[4]See G. F. Moore, loc. cit.; J. Bonsirven, Le Judaïsme
Palestinien, Vol. 1, pp. 301ff, 452ff.

[5]Ibid., p. 269.

[6]See also V. Aptowitzer, op. cit., pp. 116ff. (Notice
that the individual commandments like the Law as a totality, are
said to be eternal, see R. Marcus, op. cit., p. 53; cf. H. L.
Strack and P. Billerbeck, Kommentar, Bd. I, pp. 244ff.)

our sources was not a soil in which the belief in any radical
changes in the existing Torah was likely to grow nor a soil
which would welcome a new kind of Torah. But there are certain
preliminary factors to be noted. It is always dangerous to im-
pose any one mode of thought on Judaism: it could tolerate the
widest varieties and even contradictions of beliefs and that is
why we have placed the word "doctrine" as applied to the immutability of the Torah above in inverted commas. Moreover, it must
always be recognized that our Rabbinic sources represent the
triumph of one stream within Judaism, the Pharisaic, and even of
only one current within that one stream, that of R. Johanan b.
Zakkai.[7] Hence the possibility is always to be reckoned with
that many emphases or tendencies in Judaism in the first century
are not represented in our sources; and this is a possibility
which, in view of the antagonism which arose between the old Israel and its Torah and the new Israel with its new commandment,
is not negligible in the present enquiry: it may be that much
material in the tradition about the nature and role of Torah in
the Messianic Age has been either ignored or deliberately sup-
pressed or modified.

However, the hospitable comprehensiveness of Judaism in
matters of belief and the (possibly deliberate) comparative silence of our sources on the concept of a New Torah constitute
not evidence but merely a precaution. We must go on to enquire

---

[7]See H. Danby, The Mishnah, p. xiv f.

whether, while admitting that even in pre-Christian times the belief in the immutability of the Torah was established, there is any evidence as to another view; or are we to conclude that in the Messianic Age there would be no change in the role or character of the Torah? The following factors seem to be relevant to our discussion.

1

Our sources do reveal an awareness that, even though the Torah[8] was immutable, nevertheless modifications of various kinds, at least in certain details, would be necessary. We shall group the material as follows:

a. Passages suggesting the cessation of certain enactments concerning Festivals, etc.[9]

There were some who held the view that in the Messianic Age sin would not exist and it followed that the vast majority of sacrifices, which naturally dealt with the taint of sin,

---

[8] It is important to recognize what is meant by the Torah when we refer to its perpetuity. There are passages which claim that only the Torah in the strict sense would persist into the future: the Prophets and the Hagiographa would cease. See V. Aptowitzer, op. cit., p. 261, n. 133, who refers to Jerusalem Meg. 1, 70d; also Spiegel, H. T. R., Vol. xxiv, pp. 245ff. The passage in J. Meg. 1, 70, runs

תורה אינן עתירין ליבטל.. הנביאים והכתובים עתידין ליבטל ומשת סיפרי

[9] Translations of the B. Talmud and Midrash Rabbah, unless otherwise stated, are derived from those of the Soncino Press.

would be irrelevant.[10]   A passage in <u>Leviticus Rabbah</u> 9.7 reads:

> R. Phinehas and R. Levi and R. Johanan said in the
> name of R. Menahem of Gallia: In the time to come
> all sacrifices will be annulled, but that of Thanks-
> giving will not be annulled, and all prayers will be
> annulled, but (that of) Thanksgiving will not be
> annulled. This is (indicated by) what is written
> Jer. 33[11].

The text is:

> ר' פנחס ור' לוי ור' יוחנן בשם ר' מנחם דגל'א
> לע"ל כל הקרבנות בטלין וקרבן תודה אינו
> בטל כל התפילות בטילות התודה אינה
> בטילה הה"ד....

Here the phrase referring to the future is לעתיד לבא=לע"ל:
its meaning is fluid. Sometimes it refers to the final Age to
Come, but at other times it is equivalent to the Messianic era.[11]
The context, therefore, must decide the particular meaning it
may have: and here we are justified in referring it to the Messianic Age; the sense of the passage demands this and the verse
from Jer. 33[11] by which the view is supported comes from a Messianic prophecy. Notice, however, that the date of the view expressed must be late. Some scholars read Menahem of Galilee
reading   גליא . Israelstam[12] reads   גליא and renders

---

[10]On the place of the cultus generally in the eschatological thinking of Israel see E. Lohmeyer, <u>Kultus und Evangelium</u>,
Göttingen (1942), pp. 19ff; also pp. 49, 48ff.

[11]See M. Jastrow, <u>Dictionary of the Talmud</u>, p. 1129; J.
Bonsirven, <u>op. cit.</u>, Vol. 1, p. 319f.

[12]Soncino Translation: <u>Midrash Rabbah, Leviticus, ad loc.</u>

as above: the term אסיא he takes to refer to a place in
Asia Minor. Wünsche[13] and Loewe[14] prefer to read אסליא .
Even if we read the latter the date of the passage is 165-200
A. D. - the period when Menahem of Galilee flourished.

Another passage refers to the festivals: it comes from
<u>Yalqut</u> on Proverbs 9^2 and reads:[15]

> All the festivals will cease but not Purim (since it
> is said (Esther 9^{28}) " .... these days shall be ....
> throughout every generation .... and .... should not
> fail from among the Jews ...." R. Eleazar said: The
> Day of Atonement too will not cease since it is said
> (Lev. 16^{34}) "And this shall be unto you an everlasting
> statute."

The text runs:

כל המוצרים צתידין ליבטל וימי הפורים
אינן בטלים לצולם,.... א"ר אלצזר אף יום
הכלורים לא יבטל לצולם שנאמר והיתה זאת
לכם לחקת צולם :

The date of the passage is uncertain, but it is probably early
second century (80-120 A. D.). Here Purim and the Day of Atonement alone among the festivals are to survive into the Messianic
Age. It may be that here again we should not press the language
too closely. The justification for saying that the Day of Atonement would survive is that it is called in Leviticus 16^{34} "an

---

[13]<u>Bibliotheca Rabbinica</u>, ad <u>loc.</u>

[14]<u>Op. cit.</u>, ad <u>loc.</u>

[15]See also <u>Midrash Mishle</u>, 9.2; J. Klausner, <u>From Jesus to
Paul</u> (Eng. trans. by W. F. Stinespring), p. 321, n. 13.

everlasting statute" (חקת עולם). But the same phrase is applied elsewhere to other festivals, e.g. The Passover (Exodus 12[17]), The Feast of Weeks (Leviticus 23[21]), Tabernacles (Lev. 23[41]). It is arguable therefore that we should not take this passage at its face value, and that it is merely designed to emphasize the importance of Purim and the Day of Atonement. Nevertheless we cannot rule out the possibility that it contemplates radical changes in the festivals in the Messianic Age and is therefore significant for our purpose.[16]

b. Passages which seem to suggest changes in the laws concerning things clean and unclean, etc.

It is best to begin with a passage from Midrash Tehillim, on 146[7]. This is translated by Montefiore and Loewe[17] thus:

---

[16]D. Daube in a private communication writes: "I don't believe that the Rabbis can have been guilty of such a glaring oversight. In reality their interpretation is logical and subtle. In the texts concerning Passover, etc., the everlasting statute is limited by the addition: for your generations. The restriction is absent from Lev. 16[34]. In Esther we find, each and every generation. It is not: your generations. Moreover at the end of the sentence there is: they shall not cease from the Jews."

[17]A Rabbinic Anthology, p. 583. The date of this anonymous passage cannot be fixed. P. R. Weis, of the University of Manchester, in a private note, suggests that in view of the context the passage refers to the 'Final Age' not to the Messianic Age. The phrase לעתיד לבוא שתשכיחנה ביד"ה which occurs below the above passage, he thinks, points to this. But the conditions implied seem to us to be Messianic.

> The Lord permits the forbidden (Ps. 146[7]) [A.V. and R.V. 'looses the prisoner'; the word 'forbidden' is got by a pun]. What does this mean? Some say that in the time to come all the animals which are unclean in this world God will declare to be clean, as they were in days before Noah. And why did God forbid them [i.e., make them unclean]? To see who would accept his bidding and who would not; but in the time to come He will permit all that He has forbidden.

The text reads:

ה׳ מתיר אסורים. מהו מתיר אסורים, יש אמרים
כל הבהמה שנטמאה בעולם הזה מטהר אותה
הקב״ה לעתיד לבא....ומה שנעשה טהורים היו מקודם
לבני נח...ולמה אסר אותה, לראות מי שמקבל
דבריו, ומי אינו מקבל, ולעתיד לבוא הוא מתיר
את כל מה שאסר:

Here distinctions between clean and unclean animals are to be abrogated in the Messianic Age, which is pictured as a return to the primitive or original condition of the world before the disaster of the flood: the idea that the End corresponds to the beginning is a commonplace of Apocalyptic and the principle would seem to be operative here. But there have been objections to the acceptance of this passage as reflecting Rabbinic opinion. As Cohen pointed out,[18] Buber in a note on this passage, for a translation of which I am indebted to Israelstam, held that the phrase יש אמרים, "Some say," refers to certain unbelievers who propounded this view; moreover, following Abarbanel, he regards the passage as very late, the earliest reference to it being found in R. Moses ha - Darshan in the 10th century. We

---

[18] The Jewish Monthly, London, June, 1948, p. 186.

notice further that there is an attempt in the passage immediately following to offset the view expressed; and not only so, but it is made clear that in the time to come some of the demands of the Law would be even more severe: thus marital relations would become stricter. Nevertheless this last in itself suggests the possibility of change in the Torah, and as such is again instructive for our purpose.

It is at this point that we can best deal with a passage which is usually cited in favour not merely of the view that the Messianic Age would see changes in the Torah but also that it would bring with it a New Torah. The passage from Leviticus Rabbah 13[3] reads as follows:

> R. Judan b. R. Simeon said: Behemoth and the Leviathan are to engage in a wild beast contest before the righteous in the Time to Come, and whoever has not been a spectator at the wild beast contests of the heathen nations in this world will be accorded the boon of seeing one in the World to Come. How will they be slaughtered? Behemoth will, with its horns, pull Leviathan down and rend it, and Leviathan will, with its fins, pull Behemoth down and pierce it through. The Sages said: And is this a valid method of slaughter? Have we not learnt the following in a Mishnah: All may slaughter, and one may slaughter at all times (of the day), and with any instrument except with a scythe, or with a saw, or with teeth (in a jaw cut out of a dead animal), because they cause pain as if by choking, or with a nail (of a living body)? R. Abin b. Kahana said: The Holy One, blessed be He, said: Instruction [Torah] shall go forth from Me (Is. LI.4) i.e. an exceptional temporary ruling will go forth from Me.
> (Israelstam's Soncino translation)[19]

---

[19]V. Aptowitzer points out a parallel passage. See Jellinek, Beth ha-Midrash iii, 80; iii, 76, which reads, "In the days of the Messiah Israel will live for 2000 years in security,

The text of the last sentence according to the Wilna and Warsaw editions[19a] is:

אמ"ר אבין בר כהנא אמר הקב"ה
תורה חדשה מאתי תצא חדוש תורה מאתי תצא

Now Edersheim, like Strack-Billerbeck, who, however, qualify
their acceptance of this interpretation, took this to refer to
a new (Messianic) Torah. Israelstam, however, as we saw, rejects this, and the context favours his interpretation (see note
19a below). The point of the passage is that even though according to the Torah of this world it was not permissible to slay

---

eat from Behemoth, Leviathan, and Ziz. The Ziz and Behemoth will
be slaughtered. The Ziz will rend Leviathan and the Behemoth."
Here there is a specific reference to the days of the Messiah
when a slaughtering involving pain will be allowed, whereas in
the passage quoted in the text a painless slaughtering only will
be allowed - this because, V. Aptowitzer argues, it refers not
to the Messianic Age but to the Age to Come. But the picture of
the wild beast contest surely refers to a Messianic Age on earth,
not to the final Age to Come, in both passages.

[19a]In translating Isaiah 51:4 J. Israelstam follows the Masoretic text. It is better to understand his translation thus
than to suppose that the text of the Midrash gives the text of
Is. 51:4 last after the comment, and that Israelstam has reversed
this by giving the quotation first, then the comment. In the
1890 Warsaw edition and reprints, where there is an error by
printer or editor, the reference תצא מעשי is inserted, but in
the wrong place. It should come in front of the first תורה not
the second תורה. It is also found in some texts between תצא
and חדוש, i.e., at the end of the verse. Usually, however,
the Biblical reference is placed in front of the verse and it is
thus that J. Israelstam takes it here. He should, however, have
pointed out that he is following the Masoretic text and not that
given by the Midrash, which has the adjective חדשה. Professor A. Guttmann thinks that R. Abin bar Kahana may have had an
original text, which read חדשה. However this may be, J. Israelstam goes on to translate חדוש תורה מאתי תצא by "an
exceptional temporary ruling will go forth from me." (A. Wünsche
renders "die Erneuerung des Gesetzes wird von mir ausgehen.")
And this, as we saw above, is probably to be accepted. Professor
A. Guttmann informs me that J. Israelstam is following David
Luria who held that, הוראה החדשה in the given context means
"temporary ruling," (i.e., a ruling for the לבוא עתיד only) הוראה שעה

anything with a saw, because this would necessarily involve pain, nevertheless, in the Messianic Age the Leviathan would be permitted to pull down the Behemoth with its fins, which are like saws in that they have serrated edges. Thus in the contest between Leviathan and Behemoth, which would take place in the presence of the righteous in the Messianic Age, the use of an instrument prohibited in this world by the Torah would be allowed. This would seem to be the true understanding of the passage: the term חדש is often used of promulgating a new law (not Law) or establishing a new interpretation of a Biblical law. Thus, although it may be desireable that the element of newness in the phrase תורה חדשה should be better preserved than in Israelstam's translation, we cannot accept the passage as evidence for the expectation of a New Torah. Nevertheless, we are justified in using it as evidence for the expectation of possible changes in details of the Torah in the Messianic Age.

(c). Other passages which seem to imply or actually express the expectation of changes in the Torah.

Bonsirven refers to one passage in Siphre on Deuteronomy 17^{18}, § 160 where it is explicitly stated, he thinks, that the Torah will be changed.[20]

---

giving of Biblical references, Professor A. Guttmann notes, was not customary in the original texts of the Midrashim. Some editions do not have them, e.g., the ed. princeps, Constantinople, 1512. The second complete ed., Venice 1545, gives the references in the margin. Yet for our passage, as in the Wilna edition, no reference is given.

[20] Op. cit., Vol. 1, p. 453, n.p.   J. Klausner, op. cit., p. 54 interprets "wohl kann sie theilweise ändern (שתשתנה)

The English would roughly be as follows:

He shall write him a copy of this Law (MISHNEH HA-TORAH)
for himself. (i.e.) for his own name (person): he should
not be content with that of his fathers. MISHNEH (TORAH)
(From this) I have no (proof) except for MISHNEH TORAH
(i.e. Deuteronomy). (As to) the rest of the words of
the Torah, Whence (do we know that these too are intended)? Scripture teaches this by saying (later in this
passage) TO KEEP ALL THE WORDS OF THIS LAW, etc. Why
then (does it say) MISHNEH TORAH? Because it was des-
tined to be changed (le-Hishtannoth) - (Hithpaʿēl of
shanah, to change; also, to repeat, to copy - the root
of Mishneh).

The text reads: וכתב לו את משנה התורה הזאת
על ספר לשמו שלא יהא נאות בשל אבותיו:
משנה אין לי אלא משנה תורה שארד״ת
מנין ת״ל לשמור את כל דברי התורה הזא
א׳כ למה נאמר משנה תורה שעתידה להשתנות...

Bonsirven takes the term להשתנות to refer to a changing of

the Torah itself, and this is a perfectly legitimate possibility.

The Hithpaʿēl of שנה does mean 'to be changed': moreover, the

masculine gender of מִשְׁנֵה, makes it impossible to take

להשתנות to refer to the copy. Bonsirven's interpretation is

therefore, as stated, fully justified from the language of this

passage taken alone. Unfortunately, for our thesis, in the par-

allel passage in Tosefta, Sanhedrin 4[3ff], the phrase שעתיד ה

להשתנות   is referred quite specifically to the

change in the script which was to be used in the writing of the

Torah. The Hebrew in Tosefta, Sanhedrin 4[7] reads:

_____

שעתיד ה) aber sie kann nicht abrogirt und durch andere
ersetzt werden."

וכתבלו את משנה התורה הזאת וג'
תורה עתידה להשתנות ולמה נקרא
שמה אשורי על שום שעלה עמהן
מאשור ר' אמר בכתב אשורי
ניתנה תורה לישראל, וכשחטאו
נהפכה להן לרועץ וכשזכו בימי
עזרא חזרה להן אשורית:

The English of this would run somewhat as follows:

> And he shall write the copy of this law, etc. The
> Torah is destined to be changed. And why was it
> called[21] Assyrian script; because it went up with
> them from Assyria. R. (Meir) said: When the Torah
> was given to Israel it was given in Assyrian script;
> and when they sinned it was changed for them into
> the form of the Samaritan type, and when they were
> worthy in the days of Ezra it was renewed for them
> in Assyrian script.

The <u>Tosefta</u>, we may probably safely assume, preserves the oldest tradition of the meaning of the term להשתנות in this context, and is therefore to be followed. Hence we must reject Bonsirven's use of the passage as referring to a change in the Torah itself.

There are two other passages to be discussed here. One in <u>T. B. Sanhedrin 51b</u>, is sometimes wrongly interpreted to mean

---

[21]Reading שָׁמָה as Professor A. Guttmann advised rather than שְׁמָה . There is a variant ושמ : if we read שְׁמָה the translation is "And why was it read there in Assyrian script."

that much of the Torah which does not apply to this world will
be applicable in the Messianic Age. But the actual meaning is
that much of the Torah, meaning sacrifices, temporarily discon-
tinued in this world owing to adverse conditions, will again be
practised in the Messianic Age.[22] It reads:

> R. Nahman said in the name of Rabbah b. Abbuha in
> the name of Rab: The Halachah is in accordance with
> the message sent by Rabin in the name of R. Jose b.
> Hanina. R. Joseph queried: (Do we need) to fix a
> halachah for the days of the Messiah? - Abaye ans-
> wered: If so, we should not study the laws of sac-
> rifices, as they are also only for the Messianic
> era. But we say, Study and receive reward. i.e.
> Learning has its own merit quite apart from any
> practical utility that may be derived therefrom.

A more important and more often quoted passage occurs in
T. B. Shabbath 151b where we find opposing views set in sharp
juxtaposition. The passage reads as follows:

> R. Simeon b. Eleazar (165-200 A.D.) said: .... and
> the years draw nigh, when thou shalt say, I have no
> pleasure in them (Ecclesiastes 12¹) this refers to
> the Messianic era, wherein there is neither merit
> nor guilt. Now, he disagrees with Samuel, who said:
> The only difference between this world and the Messi-
> anic era is in respect of servitude to (foreign)
> powers, for it is said, For the poor shall never
> cease out of the land.

The context shows that the question as to when the Torah was obligatory and when it was not is the theme of the passage. Sam-
uel (first half of the third century) apparently regards the
Torah as obligatory in the Messianic Age which, he holds, would

---

[22]So A. Guttmann in a private note.

not differ in this respect from the present Age. The meaning of
R. Simeon b. Eleazar's (165-200 A.D.) dictum is difficult. Bonsirven[23] would seem to take the words to mean that in the Messianic Age the capacity to sin is obliterated, although he does
not state this explicitly and his meaning is not clear. It
seems to us that there are two possibilities as to the interpretation of the phrase חובה ולא זכות לא which is rendered
by Bonsirven, very neatly, "ni mérite ni démérite," but is better translated as "no merit and no guilt." First, the meaning
may be that in the Messianic Age the Torah will be so fully obeyed that there will be no guilt, and so spontaneously or easily
fulfilled that there will be no merit, a condition of affairs
such as Jeremiah, perhaps, may have envisaged and desiderated.
This interpretation, it will be agreed, involves a high degree
of subtlety. The second meaning is the one that seems to us perhaps most satisfying, namely, that the Torah no longer holds in
the Messianic Age, so that questions of reward for observing it
and guilt or punishment for refusing to do so do not arise. This
would make the condition of those who live in the Messianic Age,
in this respect, similar to that of the dead who, according to
R. Johanan, in the passage immediately preceding, are free from
religious duties (see below on T. B. Niddah 61b): it also implies, as we shall indicate below, that the Messianic Age is
like the Age to Come in this matter (see below, pp. 75f).

---

[23]Op. cit., Vol. 1, p. 452.

The evidence presented above sufficiently justifies the claim that despite the "doctrine" of the immutability of Torah, there were also occasional expressions of expectations that Torah would suffer modification in the Messianic Age. There were some Halakoth which would cease to be applicable in that Age; others, by contrast, would acquire a new relevance. It is important, however, to recognize explicitly that all the changes envisaged were deemed to occur within the context of the existing Torah and presuppose the continuance of its validity. Moreover, the changes contemplated imply no necessary diminution in what we may be allowed to term the severity of the yoke of the Torah. On the contrary that yoke, in some passages, was expected to become even heavier than in this age (see especially Midrash Tehillim 146[7]). In addition we have to point out that much of the traditional Christian interpretation of some of the passages cited does violence to the text and has to be rejected. It may also be helpful to state at this point that in all the passages so far quoted the reference probably is to the Messianic Age as such.

2

The second significant factor, which we have to notice, is that the Messianic Age, as indeed we might expect, is presented as an era in which certain difficulties or incomprehensibilities, which the Torah presented in this Age, would be adequately explained and comprehended: now we see in a glass darkly, but

then obscurities will be removed. Strack-Billerbeck[24] have
dealt with this, and for our purpose the briefest treatment will
suffice.

Many of the demands of the Torah seemed inexplicable and
irrational: the reasons why certain things had been forbidden or
commanded were obscure: and the fact that Jewry could not always
give a satisfying apology for much in their practice laid them
open to the attacks of Gentile cynicism and criticism. Hence
there necessarily developed a considerable activity in the Tannaitic period, as earlier probably, in an attempt to explain why
certain things had been commanded which at first seemed even
merely stupid. So eager were some to explain the טעמי תורה ,
the grounds or reasons for the Torah's demands, that they were in
danger of manipulating their texts, and consequently incurred
suspicion. The normative position arrived at was that in this
world the demands of Torah were to be obeyed because they were
commanded: this was sufficient reason for their observance. This
is made clear in the words of R. Johanan b. Zakkai (we quote the
passage from Numbers Rabbah in full because it illustrates the
kind of criticism which was made of the demands of the Torah):

An idolater asked R. Johanan b. Zakkai: These rites
that you perform look like a kind of witchcraft. You
bring a heifer, burn it, pound it, and take its ashes.
If one of you is defiled by a dead body you sprinkle
upon him two or three drops and you say to him: "Thou

[24]Op. cit., Vol. IV, p. 2, n. 9; see for a convenient review of the most recent treatment M. Waxman, J. Q. R., New Series, Vol. XLII, October, 1951, on Taame Ha-Mitzwot.

art clean." R. Johanan asked him: 'Has the demon
of madness ever possessed you?' 'No!' he replied.
'Have you ever seen a man possessed by this demon
of madness?' 'Yes,' said he. 'An what do you do
in such a case?' 'We bring roots,' he replied,
'and make them smoke under him, then we sprinkle
water upon the demon and it flees.' Said R. Johanan to him: 'Let your ears hear what you utter
with your mouth: Precisely so is this spirit a
spirit of uncleanness: as it is written, And also
I will cause the prophets and the unclean spirit
to pass out of the land (Zech. XIII, 2). Water
of purification is sprinkled upon the unclean and
the spirit flees.' When the idolater had gone R.
Johanan's disciples said to their master: 'Master'
This man you have put off with a mere makeshift
but what explanation will you give to us? Said he
to them: 'By your life.' It is not the dead that
defiles nor the water that purifies! The Holy One,
blessed be He, merely says: "I have laid down a
statute (חקה)25, I have issued a decree. You
are not allowed to transgress My decree;" as it is
written, "This is the statute of the law" (Num.
XIX, 2).

But although theirs was not to reason why in this world,
the Rabbis were convinced that the Messianic Age would bring
with it an explanation of the inexplicable demands that the Torah
made in this world: the טעמי תורה would be revealed.26 We
have previously quoted passages from the Old Testament where the
Messianic Age was depicted as a time when God himself would
teach His people. This was the firm conviction of the Rabbis
also. In illustration we shall again quote a passage from Numbers Rabbah XIX. 6, despite its late date, where the reference

---

25This term denotes a command demanding implicit obedience,
though the human mind may not comprehend its reason.

26See what was written on pp. 42f, above concerning the
Teacher of Righteousness.

is not strictly to the Messianic Age, however, but to the final Age to Come.

> "That they bring Thee a Red Heifer (XIX. 2). R. Jose b. Hanina (the second half of the third century) expounded: The Holy One, blessed be He, said to Moses: To thee I shall disclose the reason for the Heifer, but to anybody else it is a statute." For R. Huna said: It is written, when I take the appointed time, (i.e., in the World to Come), I Myself will judge with equity (Ps. LXXV. 3) (i.e., reveal the reasons for My Laws), and it is also written, And it shall come to pass in that day, that there shall not be light, but heavy clouds and thick - Wekippa'on (Zech. 14⁶). The written form is 'Yekippa'on,' as much as to say: The things that are concealed from you in this world, you will see in the World to Come, like a blind man who regains his sight; as it is written (Isaiah 42¹⁶), And I will bring the blind by a way that they know not 27

It is not necessary to enlarge further on this point and we pass on to the next group of material.

3

Despite the changes both in the substance and interpretation of the Torah which they contemplate, those passages which

---

27Sh. Spiegel, H. T. R., October, 1931, p. 261, points out that part of the significance of the predicted coming of Elijah on the threshold of the Messianic Age was that he should settle legal and ritual doubts "to set straight all dissension, and to compose differences of opinion which could threaten to make of the one law two laws." He relates this function of Elijah to the doctrine of the perpetual validity of the Law: the difficulties of the existing Law had to be explained because there could be no other Law. Hence the great joy of the Rabbis at being able to resolve contradictions between Ezekiel and the Torah: they feared the danger of having to admit the existence of two laws in the canon should these contradictions not be resolved. Cp. H. Danby, op. cit., p. 12, n. 4 on M. Eduyoth 8.7.

we have so far examined have afforded no evidence for the expectation of a New Torah in the Messianic Age. Changes in details
and an increase in understanding there would be, but no substi-
tution of the old Torah by a new one was envisaged. In this
section we must deal with passages where it has been claimed
that it is possible that a New Torah is expressly indicated. But
first we must recall that Leviticus Rabbah 13³, although frequent-
ly cited in this connection as referring to a New Torah, probably does not in fact contain this concept, and must therefore
be passed by. The other passages which fall to be considered
are the following:

1. The Targum on Isaiah 12³ which reads:

ותתבלין אולפן חדת בחדוא
מבחירי צדיקיא :

"And you shall receive a new teaching with
joy from the chosen of Righteousness."

The term תורה is not used but the idea is clear that a new
kind of instruction will be given; and Daube²⁸ accepts אולפן

---

²⁸J. T. S., Vol. XXXIX. To this M. Jastrow lends support,
op. cit., p. 26. In the Targum on Isaiah 23 and 32⁶ אולפן
and אוריתא are parallel. Dr. Daube takes the phrase
אולפן חדת of this passage to mean "that Israel will be
given a better Law, a new and final revelation." (Ibid., p. 55.)
It is equivalent to תורה חדשה , but this term, he thinks,
was probably "used much more loosely in colloquial speech than
it would seem from that particular passage in Targum." He refers
to Tos. Sotah 14¹ to prove that " תורה does not necessarily
signify the unique, ideal Law laid down by God. It may mean the
Law as understood by one of the various sects; any of them might
claim to have the true Torah, in contrast to the Torah of the

as the equivalent of תורה here: the drawing of water out of the wells of salvation (Isaiah 12³ ᶠᶠ) is equated with the reception of new teaching. Water, of course, is a familiar figure for the Torah.[29]

2. <u>Midrash Qoheleth 2¹ and 12¹</u>

In the passage, <u>Midrash Qoheleth 12¹</u>, we read:

תורה שאדם למד בעוה"ז
הבל היא לפי תורה של משיח :

"The Torah which a man learnt in this world is
vanity compared with the Torah of the Messiah."

This passage carries no date; a somewhat similar passage which is given in the name of R. Simon b. Zabdai, but slightly more involved, is that in 2¹, which is as follows:

ר' חזקיה בש"ר סימון בר זבדי אמר כל
התורה שאת למד בעוה"ז הבל היא לפני
תורה שבעוה"ב. לפי שבעוה"ז אדם
לומד ושכח אבל לעתיד לבא מה
כתיב תמן... נתתי את תורתי בקרבכם :

---

opponents. It follows that when Jesus added yet another doctrine to those already in existence, he may well have been regarded as founder of a תורה חדשה ." Daube takes διδαχή καινή in Mark 1²⁷ to mean הלכה חדשה or הרי׳ה חדשה or again תלמוד חדשה . The whole article is of first rate importance.

[29] H. L. Strack - P. Billerbeck, <u>op. cit.</u>, Band II, p. 433.

> R. Hezekiah said in the name of Rabbi Simon bar Zabdai:
> All the Torah which you learn in This world is vanity
> compared with the Torah in The world to Come. For in
> This world a man learns and forgets but, as for The
> time to come, what is written there (Jer. 31^{33})? I
> have given my Law in their inward parts.

The date of R. Simon b. Zabdai is late (circa 300 A. D.). But

the passage is interesting on more grounds than one. Not only

does it help us to understand how the Rabbis understood the Law

of the New Covenant of Jeremiah, i.e. as referring to the Mosaic

Torah, but its context also reveals the background against which

we are to place discussions of the problem of the future role of

the Torah; because it is noteworthy that in the previous section

R. Phinehas (fourth century A. D.) had referred both to the

words of the Torah and to the words of מִינוּת , (heresy), that

is, of sectaries, probably Jewish Christians. Then follows the

passage quoted above, the contrast between Torah in This world

and that of The world to come: whereas in This world men learn

and forget Torah, in The world to come they will learn and not

forget; the Torah of God will be in their hearts. The polemic

background of the saying is significant, and will occupy us in

due course. Now at first sight it would appear that the phrase

תורה של משיח in 12^1 implies a contrast between the

תורה of This world and that of The world to come, but as Pro-

fessor A. Guttmann noted to the author, 12^1 is to be interpreted

in the light of 2^1. The תורה של משיח , he thinks, is

to be understood as "the Torah of the days of the Messiah." And

even if this be not admitted, it is not the Torah that is to be

changed in The Age to Come (= the Messianic Age here), but the relation of man to the Torah: i.e. the Torah will then be differently and more satisfactorily studied.

3. <u>Targum</u> <u>on</u> <u>Song</u> <u>of</u> <u>Songs</u> 5[10]:

דודי בכן שריתא כנשתא דישראל למשתעי
בשבחא למרי עלמא וכן אמרת ההוא אלהא
רעותי למפלח דעטיף ביממא באעטלא חור
כתלגא וזיו יקרא דיי דאנפוהי זהרק כנורא
מסגיאות חוכמתא וסברא דהוא מחדת
שמוצין חדתין בכל יומא ועתיד לפרסמנון
לעמיה ביומא רבא וסיפסיה על רבוא רבן מלאכין
דמשמשין קדמוי :

The English would run somewhat as follows:

My beloved (Cant. 5[10]). Then K[e]nesseth Israel commences to engage in the praise of the Master of the Universe and speaks thus: "It is my delight to worship God who wraps Himself by day in a robe white as snow and the glorious divine splendour whose countenance shines like a flame by reason, greatness of wisdom, and thought, who delivers anew every day new traditions (or decisions) which He is to make known to His people on the Great Day, and whose array (or royal authority) extends over myriads and myriads of angels who serve before Him."

Here Strack-Billerbeck refer, in a paraphrase of the above, to new <u>Halakoth</u> which God will give <u>by</u> <u>the</u> <u>hand</u> of the Messiah. But the text does not include a reference to the Messiah. The thought expressed is that new interpretations showing a new ingenuity in exegesis of the Torah will be given in "the great day" by God himself.

4. <u>Yalqut</u> <u>on</u> <u>Isaiah</u> <u>26</u>.

This passage we may translate as follows:

The Holy One, blessed be He, will sit in Paradise and give instruction (דורש), and all the righteous will sit before him and all the hosts (lit. family) of Heaven will stand on His right and the sun, and stars on His left; and the Holy One, blessed be He, interprets (דורש) to them the grounds of a new Torah (תורה חדשה) which the Holy One, blessed be He, will give to them by the hand of King Messiah.

The Hebrew of the last sentence reads:

והקב״ה דורש להם טעמי תורה חדשה

שעתיד הקב״ה ליתן להם על יד מלך המשיח:

This seems to be the most unambiguous reference to a new Messianic Torah. Jewish scholars, however, have pointed out that Abarbanel's reading apparently was

טעמי מצוות ע״ד מלך המשיח

i.e., "grounds of commandments by the hand of King Messiah." But we can see why such an explicit reference to a new Messianic Torah would naturally lead to uneasiness, and possibly give rise to a modified and safer reading. Moreover, the attempt[30] to interpret the phrase טעמי תורה חדשה as if it meant טעמי תורה החדשים, i.e., "new grounds of Torah," is suspect for the same reasons. It is not, therefore, impossible to find in this passage an explicit reference to a Messianic Torah, new in kind.

---

[30] J. Israelstam in a private note thought this a remote possibility.

5. Song of Songs Rabbah 2¹³.

A passage which Klausner discussed is that found in Song
of Songs Rabbah 2¹³ on the words: "The fig tree putteth forth
her green figs." The whole passage reads as follows:

> R. Johanan said: As for the seven years in which the
> Son of David comes: the first year will see estab-
> lished what is written (Amos 4) "And I caused it to
> rain upon one city, etc." In the second arrows of
> hunger shall be sent upon it: in the third a great
> famine and men and women and children will die, and
> the pious and the men of "good works" will be dimin-
> ished: and the Torah will be forgotten from Israel:
> in the fourth there will be hunger and no hunger:
> plenty and no plenty: in the fifth a great plenty:
> and they shall eat and drink and rejoice and the
> Torah shall return to its renewal and it will be
> renewed to Israel.

אֵ"ר יוחנן שבוע שבן דוד בא שנה ראשונה מתקיים
מה שנאמ'(עמוס ד) והמטרתי על עיר אחת וגו'.בשניה
חצי רעב משתלחין בה . בשלישית רעב גדול ומתים
בו אנשים ונשים ופף, וחסידים ואנשי מעשה מתמעטים.
והתורה משתכחת מישראל. ברבי'עי רעב ולא
רעב. שובע ולא שובע. בחמישית שובע גדול.
ואוכלין ושותין ושמחין .והתורה חוזרת לחדושה
ומתחדשת לישראל:

In his discussion of this Klausner insists that the idea
that the Torah would be forgotten from Israel in the days preceding the advent of the Messiah is early and that the phrase

והתורה חוזרת לחדושה ומתחדשת לישראל:

is really a late alteration of words which originally meant that
in the days of the Messiah the Torah, which had been forgotten,

would return to those learning it.[31] (See <u>Sanhedrin 97a</u>.) He
objects to the whole passage as a very late one. And it must be
admitted that, even if we do take it literally, the phrase
חוזרת לחידושה may merely mean, as Klausner insists, "will
return to its original state," so that it does not refer to a
New Torah which will replace the old, and this latter meaning
can only be regarded as a very remote possibility.[32]

4

There remains one other aspect of Torah in the Messianic
Age which should be noted very briefly. There are passages
which anticipate that the Gentiles will come to share in the
blessings of the Torah in the Messianic Age. This was expressed
in the Old Testament passages which we discussed and it is taken
up by the Rabbis. The chief passage is in <u>Genesis Rabbah 98</u>:

> He washeth his garments in wine (Gen. 49[11]) intimates
> that He (The Messiah) will make clear (שהוא מתירר להם
> ד"ת) for them words of Torah; And his vesture
> in the blood of grapes - that He will make clear to them
> their errors. (שהוא מתיר להם טעויה) R. Hanin
> said: Israel will not require the teaching (התלמוד של
> מלך המשיה) of the royal Messiah in the future,

---

[31]<u>Op. cit.</u>, p. 53; J. Klausner points out that in the parallel passage <u>Pesiqta 75a</u> (Ed. M. Friedmann) the words ומתחדשת
לישראל are missing. He rejects Weiss' view that the change
from והתורה וומדיה חוזרת ללהתורה to התורה חוזרת לחידושה
is early. R. Johanan died in 279 A. D. In <u>Pesiqta</u> the passage
is cited in the name of רבנן : the partial parallel in <u>San-
hedrin 97a</u> is anonymous.

[32]V. Aptowitzer, <u>op. cit.</u>, compares the phrase with that
used to describe the new moon, לבנה בחידושה , <u>Sanhe-
drin 42a</u>.

for it says, Unto him shall the nations seek (Is. XI[10]), but not Israel. If so, for what purpose will the royal Messiah come, and what will He do. He will come to assemble the exiles of Israel and to give them (the Gentiles) thirty precepts (מצות) as it says, And I said unto them: If ye think good, give me my hire: and if not, forbear. So they weighed for my hire thirty pieces of silver (Zech. XI, 12). Rab. said: This alludes to thirty mighty men. R. Johanan said: It alludes to thirty precepts (i.e. which the Gentiles will undertake to observe when the Messiah comes). R. Johanan's disciples said to him: Does not Rab hold that the verse refers only to the nations of the world? - In Rab's view, 'And I said unto them' means unto Israel, while in R. Johanan's view 'And I said unto them' means unto the nations of the world ....

So Genesis Rabbah 98.8 reads:

Until Shiloh cometh: this alludes to the royal Messiah. And unto Him shall the obedience of the people be: he (the Messiah) will come and set on edge the teeth of the nations of the world.

The first passage seems to imply both that the Messiah will bring His teaching and that He will propound new meanings and interpretations of Torah, but that He will direct all this to the nations not to Israel, because the latter, presumably, will receive its teaching directly from God, or already had received the requisite teaching.

There were different views as to what demands would be made on the Gentiles: according to some all the minute details of the Torah would be imposed upon them: according to Midrash Tehillim, 31[1] only three ordinances would be binding upon them: according to others the Noachian commandments would be placed upon them. We need not here enlarge on the details: it is the

fact that is significant that in the opinion of some Rabbis at
least the Gentiles would submit to the yoke of the Torah in the
Messianic Age.[33]

5

So far we have discussed what role the Torah was expected
to play in the Messianic Age in a strict sense, and in particular whether Jewish speculation contemplated a New Torah in that
Age. We have dealt with the relevant material in the light of
the 'doctrine' of the immutability of the Torah which almost
dominated Judaism. Next we have to refer to passages which have
been held to suggest not merely that there would be changes in
the Torah in the Messianic Age but that it would be completely
abrogated.

The chief passage comes from T. B. Sanhedrin 97b and
Abodah Zarah 9b; it reads:

> The Tanna debe Eliyyahu taught: The world is to exist
> six thousand years: the first two thousand years are
> to be void; the next two thousand years are the period
> of the Torah; and the following two thousand years are
> the period of the Messiah.

The meaning of The Tanna debe Eliyyahu in this connection
is defined by Mishcon[34] as "a Midrash containing chiefly

---

[33]See A. Edersheim, op. cit., Vol. II, pp. 764ff; unfortunately there is no attempt made to date the various passages
listed.

[34]Soncino Translation of T. B. Abodah Zarah, ad loc.

Baraithas compiled by R. Anan, Bab. Amora of the 3rd cent." We
may therefore conclude that the evidence it supplies is fairly
early. Baeck[35] on the strength of this, and other passages of
lesser importance, has concluded that "At that time (i.e. the
first century), the belief was widespread among the Jews that
world history consisted of three epochs: first, the period of
chaos - tohubohu; then the period of the Torah, beginning with
the revelation on Mount Sinai; and finally, the hoped-for period
of the Messiah .... In conformity with this, the Gospels say:
"Till heaven and earth pass, one jot or one tittle shall in no
wise pass from the law, till all be fulfilled" (Matt. 5:18). When
all is fulfilled, and the Messiah has come, the period of the
law will have come to its close." The same position is maintained by Silver.[36] Freedman, however, rejects this interpretation
of the passage from The Tanna debe Eliyyahu, and comments on the
reference to the period of the Torah that: "This does not mean
that the Torah shall cease thereafter, but is mentioned merely
to distinguish it from the next era."[37] Mishcon makes no reference to the problem posed by the passage.

But we have seen that there is a passage in T. B. Shabbath 151b, which possibly offers some support for Baeck's

---

[35]The Pharisees, pp. 72f.

[36]The History of Messianic Speculation in Israel (1927),
p. 9.

[37]Soncino Translation of T. B. Sanhedrin, Vol. II, p. 657,
n. 9.

interpretation, where it is stated that in the Messianic Age there would be neither merit nor guilt (זכות ולא חובה אל). Baeck also refers to T. B. Niddah 61b to confirm his position. It reads:

אמר רב יוסף זאת אומרת מצוות בטלות
לעתיד לבא:

i.e. R. Joseph said: "This means the commandments shall be abrogated in The time to come." Baeck refers this passage to the Messianic Age, but the context makes it clear that the reference is to the condition of the dead, who, as we have seen before, are not subject to the Torah. The point at issue in T. B. Niddah 61b is that of the use of sha'atnez, i.e., a mixture of wool and linen, which was prohibited to the living but, because death brings exemption from mitzwoth, was nevertheless, permitted as shrouds for the dead. It seems clear, therefore, that in this passage the phrase לעתיד לבא merely means 'in death,' and it is difficult to agree either with Klausner[38] that the context of T. B. Niddah 61b supports the view that the saying does not merely refer to life in the next world but also, by implication, to the Messianic Age, or with Baeck who refers it expressly to the Messianic Age. But, that the idea contained in T. B. Niddah 61b may refer to the Age to Come and not merely to the life after death is highly probable, if not certain. It may be permissible for us to refer here to our argument in Paul and Rabbinic

---

[38] Jesus of Nazareth (English trans.), p. 275; Klausner regards the passage as earlier than R. Joseph.

Judaism[39] that the Age to Come was regarded both as an event,
which came into being in time, and also as an eternally exist-
ent reality in the heavens, as it were. Hence, in one sense,
one entered the Age to Come at death when one became free from
the obligation to obey the mitzwoth; this is what T. B. Niddah
61b explicitly refers to; but in another sense the Age to Come
was to come into history and when this would happen the mitzwoth
would also cease then, and by implication T. B. Niddah 61b can
be referred to this Age to Come that is to come. We can only refer T. B. Niddah 61b to the Messianic Age if we can equate or
identify this (i.e., the Messianic Age) with the Age to Come.
That this is a justifiable equation would seem reasonable in many
passages: we have seen above that the phrase לעתיד לבא was
very fluid and could refer both to the Messianic Age and to the
final Age to Come, i.e. the post Messianic period. The distinction between the Age to Come and the Messianic Age is a compara-
tively late development, and it follows that they were often
synonymous terms in early Apocalyptic.[40] On the other hand, however, there are passages where the Messianic Age and the Age to
Come are sharply distinguished: of the former it was possible to
prophecy, but of the latter it was thought that it transcended
all human conception. A passage in T. B. Shabbath 63b makes

---

[39]Pp. 314ff.

[40]See R. H. Charles, Eschatology, pp. 200f, and especially
J. Klausner, Die Messianischen Vorstellungen des jüdischen Volkes
im Zeitalter der Tannaiten, pp. 17ff.

this clear:

> Samuel said, This world differs from the Messianic
> Era only in respect to servitude of the exiled; for
> it is said, For the poor shall never cease out of
> the land. This supports R. Hiyya b. Abba, who said,
> All the prophets prophesied only for the Messianic
> Age, but as for The world to come, the eye hath not
> seen O Lord, beside thee what he hath prepared for
> him that waiteth for him 41

In view therefore of the distinction between the Messianic Age
and the Age to Come implied and explicitly stated in such passages as this, it is probably highly precarious to apply T. B.
Niddah 61b too surely to the Messianic Age as such. We can only be sure from this passage that in the Age to Come, that Age
that both IS and COMES, the mitzwoth will cease, but we can only regard this as a possibility for the Messianic Age. This
point is important for the understanding of the New Testament;
and the question forces itself whether the distinction of This
Age and The Age to Come had come to clear expression in the
time of Jesus. This is discussed by Volz, op. cit., pp. 63ff.
He concludes that the idea of the Two Ages in any case is older
than the terms used to express it; we may safely assume that
the distinction was a real one in the time of Jesus.[42] Bon-

---

41See T. W. Manson, The Teaching of Jesus[2], p. 277, n. 2:
cp. I Cor. 29.

42The significance of this for the New Testament will be
clear when we recognise that the difficulty of deciding whether
Paul, for example, believed that in the Resurrection of Jesus
the final Age to Come had come or whether that event merely in-
augurated the Messianic Age has an important bearing on Paul's

sirven[43] thinks that the expressions הזה העולם and

הבא העולם[44] appeared at that time.

---

attitude to the Law, just as the same difficulty must influence our interpretation of Mt. 5[18]. The difficulty is such, however, that we cannot pursue it here. For Paul, see W. D. Davies, Paul and Rabbinic Judaism (1948), pp. 297f. Since this book was published, however, H. J. Schoeps in Aus Frühchristlicher Zeit: Religionsgeschichtliche Untersuchungen (Tübingen, 1950), has dealt with this very point under the title Paulus als rabbinischer Exeget, 1. Χριστὸς Τέλος νόμου, pp. 221ff. He applies some of the passages which we have examined above to the phrase in Rom. 10[4]. "Die Geltung des Gesetzes als göttlichen Heilsweges ist seit der Auferstehung Jesu von den Toten, die seine Messianität sowohl wie auch den Anbruch der Endzeit beweist, beendigt. Denn 'das Gesetz ist Herr über den Menschen, solange er lebt' (Rom. 7[1])" (p. 223). In view of our treatment, however, H. J. Schoeps' conclusions would seem to be much too bold.

[43] Op. cit., Vol. 1, p. 312.

[44] N. Messel, in Die Einheitlichkeit der jüdischen Eschatologie (1915), disputed the view that Jewish Eschatology contained the distinction between This (earthly) Age and the (supernatural) Age to Come. The terms refer throughout according to him to a purely this worldly and earthly conception. See P. Volz, ibid., p. 66.

V

CONCLUSION AND ITS RELATION TO THE NEW TESTAMENT

In the passages treated above we have sought to discover that part the Torah was expected to play in the ideal future whether conceived as a Messianic Age or as the ultimate Age to Come. To recapitulate, we found in the Old Testament, the Apocrypha and Pseudepigrapha and in the Rabbinical sources the profound conviction that obedience to the Torah would be a dominating mark of the Messianic Age, and in the prophet Jeremiah a certain tension as to whether this obedience would be spontaneous in the sense that it would not be directed to, nor governed by, any external code, or whether some form of external Torah would still be operative. Generally, however, our sources revealed the expectation that the Torah in its existing form would persist into the Messianic Age when its obscurities would be made plain, and when there would be certain natural adaptations and changes and, according to some, the inclusion of the Gentiles among those who accepted the yoke of the Torah. It turned out to be difficult always to distinguish the Messianic Age from the Age to Come in the final sense, but we found evidence for the belief that this last would transcend all human thought and see the cessation of mitzwoth: but since the Holy One Himself was conceived to be occupied with the study of the Torah in the eternal world, we must not preclude the Torah even from the Age to Come in too radical a fashion.[1]

---

[1] See G. F. Moore, Judaism, Vol. I, p. 273.

85

The evidence for the expectation of a New Torah which the
Messiah should bring was not sufficiently definite and unambiguous to make us as certain as were Edersheim and Dalman[2] that
this was a well defined and accepted element in the Messianic
hope, but neither was it inconsiderable and questionable enough
for us to dismiss it, as does Klausner, as merely a late development in a Judaism influenced by Christianity, a point to which
we shall return later. Strack-Billerbeck's claim that the Torah
of the Messiah would be new merely in the sense that it would
expound the old Torah more fully than was possible in This Age
probably errs on the side of caution. We can at least affirm
that there were elements inchoate in the Messianic hope of Judaism, which could make it possible for some to regard the Messianic Age as marked by a New Torah, new indeed, as Strack-Billerbeck maintain, not in the sense that it contravened the old,
but yet not merely in the sense that it affirmed the old on a
new level, but in such a way as to justify the adjective חדשה
that was applied to it. (Possibly Jeremiah would have thought
of a Torah new in kind, but even he, as we suggested, did not
exclude the possibility of this new kind of Torah having at the
same time an element of gramma in it like that of the old Torah).

It is perilously easy, however, to systematize what was
vague and amorphous. Moreover, the isolation of passages dealing with one theme and their presentation in a concentrated,

---

[2]Jesus-Jeshua,(English trans.,),(1929), p. 85.

consecutive manner can too easily create an erroneous impression of their significance: to isolate in this context is to magnify: and to view the passages with which we have dealt in true perspective it is necessary to set them over against the vast continent of the Rabbinical sources; only then can they be rightly assessed. Nor must it be forgotten that the passages which we have cited are all haggadic, so that they must lack a certain seriousness which more halakic passages would afford.[3]

In addition to all this, there is one difficulty, which we mentioned at the beginning of our discussion, which we have not yet met. Those passages which specifically use the term תורה חדשה are late; and Klausner, who apparently accepts this term as referring to a New Torah, claims that the passages concerned are the result of Christian influence, by way of reaction, of course, upon Judaism. At a date earlier than these passages what we usually find is the belief that, before the Messianic Age, Torah would almost fail in Israel but that it would later return. This late date of the passages, it is clear, is a real difficulty, no less than the paucity of their number, but we can submit certain considerations which may serve to offset these two factors.

First, we must emphasize again that the silence of our sources as to an early belief in a New Torah may be due to deliberate surgery. We have previously pointed out that our

---

[3]G. F. Moore, op. cit., Vol. I, p. 162.

Rabbinic sources represent merely the Pharisaic element in Judaism and that certain polemic tendencies are traceable in them. We do know that the question of the New Torah agitated Judaism. There is a passage in Deuteronomy Rabbah 8 which reads thus:

> It is written, 'For this commandment is not in heaven' (Deut. XXX. 11, 12). Moses said to the Israelites, Lest you should say, Another Moses is to arise, and to bring us another Law from heaven, therefore I make it known to you now that it is not in heaven: nothing of it is left in heaven ....

The polemical intention is obvious. Paul had used the same kind of midrash on Deuteronomy 30^{14} in Rom. 10^{6ff} in support of the view that Christ, God's word, had drawn near to men. Again in Baruch 3^{29ff} we hear another undertone of controversy where Wisdom is claimed to be inaccessible in the following terms:

> Who hath gone up into heaven, and taken her
> (i.e., Wisdom).
> And brought her down from the clouds?
> Who hath gone over the sea, and found her
> And will bring her for choice gold?

Justin's Dialogue with Trypho makes the same controversy clear: he goes so far as to claim that he has read that there will be a final Law.[4]

---

[4]Ante-Nicene Christian Library, Vol. II, see pp. 99f. Justin here claims that he has read "that there shall be a final law (and an eternal one)." Νυνὶ δὲ ἀνέγνων γάρ, ὦ Τρύφων, ὅτι ἔσοιτο καὶ τελευταῖος νόμος καὶ Διαθήκη κυριωτάτη

88

Weiss[5] also regarded the following passage from T. B. Shabbath 104a, which claims that the text of the Torah can suffer no innovations from any prophet, as directed against Paul's attitude towards the Torah. The phrase 'these are the commandments, derived from Lev. 27³⁴ were taken to teach that' "a prophet may hence forth (i.e., after Moses) make no innovations;" and Strack-Billerbeck cite R. Johanan b. Zakkai's famous dictum, which we cited above, p.67f, as a direct polemic comment on Mk. 7¹⁴ff (and parallels).[6] In view of all the above, we may safely claim that the early presentation of Christianity as involving a New Law in the Sermon on the Mount or in the Kainê entolê of the Fourth Gospel produced counter claims within Judaism such as we see in Deuteronomy Rabbah 8. But this may also perhaps account for the absence in our Rabbinic sources of any specific early references to a New Torah, such as may possibly have been once contemplated. By the time that those passages which actually speak of a New Torah are found, the separation of Church and Synagogue had become such that speculation among Jews and Christians could be mutually stimulating without being dangerous. It

πλσῶν... Αἰώνιος τε ἡμιν νόμος (Is. LV,3; LXI,8; Jer xxxii,40) καὶ τελευταῖος ὁ Χριστὸς ἐδόθη καὶ ἡ διαθήκη πιστή.

Text from G. Archambault, Justin Dialogue avec Tryphon, Paris, 1909, Tome I, pp. 51ff. See especially n. 2.

[5] Cited in Soncino Translation of T. B. Shabbath, ad loc.

[6] H. L. Strack - P. Billerbeck, Kommentar, Vol. I, p. 719.

is arguable, at least, that this might account for the greater readiness of later Judaism to speak of a New Torah.[7]

Secondly, a further similar consideration illustrates the kind of situation which may account for the absence of early references to any New Torah. It has been pointed out by Bonsirven that despite the fact that the idea of the Covenant dominates Jewish thought, surprisingly enough the idea is relatively little exploited in the Rabbinical sources. Bonsirven gives a reason for this: he rightly suggests that the Law had replaced it as the centre of Jewish life and thought;[8] but an additional reason

---

[7]I have here followed J. Klausner, but I do so with hesitation. I am not quite sure that he is correct in thinking that it would be easier for later Judaism to contemplate a New Torah than it would have been for first century Judaism. The antipathy to Christianity had become greater, not less. The concept of a New Torah might perhaps have been indigenous and not merely the outcome of Christian influences.

[8]Op. cit., Vol. I, pp. 79f. His words deserve quotation. "Cette idée de l'alliance domine toute la pensée juive: nous sommes d'autant plus surpris de constater que la litterature rabbinique a relativement peu exploité cette donnée biblique primordiale." J. Bonsirven asserts that there are very few places where Rabbis speculate on the Covenantal idea: in the Midrashim comments on the Biblical texts dealing with the Covenant are few. He also points out how sectarian movements remained far truer to the Old Testament in this; e.g., the Damascus Sect governed its life on the covenantal principle. Thus not only Christian concentration on covenantal ideas, but other sectarian tendencies also would tend to reinforce the surprising neglect of the explicit treatment of such texts in the Rabbinic sources. To judge from the extant works of Philo the same neglect of the covenantal idea might be found in Hellenistic Judaism, but G. F. Moore pointed out that Philo wrote two lost treatises on the Covenants (see R. Marcus, [citing G. F. Moore,] op. cit., p. 14, n.). (The view expressed by H. J. Schoeps in Aus Frühchristlicher Zeit, p. 228 that Diaspora Judaism or Septuagint-Judaism, as he describes it, had a false conception of

for the fact mentioned surely may be that the covenantal idea
was so prominent in Christianity that it became, if not exactly
distasteful to Judaism, nevertheless deliberately disused because of its marked Christian associations. It is the same kind
of reaction against the New Law preached by early Christians
which may have caused the comparative silence of the Rabbinic
sources on the concept of a New Law.

The evidence that we have been able to adduce in favour
of a new Messianic Torah cannot be regarded as very impressive.
But what makes it probable that some elements in Judaism at least
may have contemplated a new Messianic Torah is the fact that
early Christians, who were conscious that they were living in
the Messianic Age, did in fact find room in their interpretation
of the Christian Dispensation for such a concept. At this point

---

the Covenantal relation between Yahweh and Israel, as did also
Paul, to speak very midly, is to be very seriously questioned.)
H. J. Schoeps, Theologie und Geschichte des Judenchristentums,
p. 90, offers parallels to the above mentioned neglect of the
covenant concept in the Rabbis, parallels which are illuminating.
Schoeps is concerned to show the way in which Judaism reacted to
the Jewish-Christian emphasis on Christ as the New Moses. He
writes: "Welchen Rang und welche Verbreitung dieses Dogma, viel-
leicht auf essaïsche Ursprunge zurückgehend, Christus Jesus -
Novus Moses in der jüdischen Christenheit gehabt haben muss,
lassen uns auch zwei weitere Umstände erkennen .... Zum anderen
der auffällige Verzicht der Tannaiten und frühen Amoräer, Deut.
18.15 und 18 auszulegen [see especially p. 90, n. 3 for evi-
dence]. Es begegnet uns hier dieselbe Erscheinung wie bei der
Auslegungsgeschichte von Jes. 53, Ps. 2.7, 110.1; Jer. 31, 31f;
Hosea 2.25 usw. Die jüdische Theologie der ersten Jahrhunderte
n. Chr. fand diese Schriftstellen bereits durch die Christliche
Auslegung präokkupiert und verzichtete daher auf ihre erwendung
innehalb messianischer Diskussionen oder legte sie betont un-
eschatologisch aus." (Our italics.) Cf. also G. Quell, Theologisches Wörterbuch, Band 11, ad loc. For the way in which

we must insist that the New Testament must be allowed to illumine the Messianic hope of Judaism. It is surely a striking and significant fact that the New Testament presents Christianity, among other things, as a movement which not only denies the old Torah on one level, and affirms and fulfils it on another, but also introduces a New Torah.

In this connection the evidence garnered above has both a negative and positive aspect. First, as we wrote at the beginning, could we clearly distinguish the role expected of the Torah in the Messianic Age and in The Age to Come in the eschatological speculation of first century Judaism we would be able to set the early Christian attitude to the Law in true perspective. Thus by determining how the various elements in the New Testament regarded the Resurrection, whether, that is, it was regarded as the inauguration of the Messianic Age or of the Age to Come proper in its ultimate manifestation, we could then discover what attitude to the Law would be natural to them. But this our Jewish sources will not allow us to do, except in the most ambiguous way. Not only was the distinction between the Age to Come and the Messianic Age not always clearly defined so that we had constant difficulty in deciding to which Age a particular passage referred, but it would not be correct to speak

---

Judaism closed its ranks against Christianity see S. W. Baron, A social and religious history of the Jews², Vol. II, Part II, Philadelphia, 1952, pp. 130ff, and the bibliographical details he supplies.

of any one generally accepted Jewish expectation as to the role
of the Torah in either of these two periods. The result of our
survey in this respect must be regarded as negative.

But, in the second place, there is a further positive
result. We may with some confidence assert that the Gospel of
Matthew regards the words of Jesus as a New Torah; and tended to
find in them the ground for a new halakah. The words of Jesus
'fulfilled' the Law and the Prophets, they were the Torah of the
Messiah. Similarly Paul too found in the words of Jesus the basis of a new halakah: In fact he used the phrase - the Law of
the Messiah (οὕτως ἀναπληρώσατε τὸν νόμον τοῦ
Χριστοῦ [תורה של משיח], Gal. 6²).[9] Similarly the
Fourth Gospel not only speaks of the ἐντολαὶ τοῦ Χριστοῦ
(14¹⁵), but also of the Καινὴ ἐντολή (13³⁴).[10] In

---

[9]See W. D. Davies, Paul and Rabbinic Judaism, 1948, pp.
141ff; and especially O. Cullmann, Revue d'histoire et de phi-
losophie religieuses, No. 1 (1950), pp. 12ff; also Morton Smith,
Tannaitic Parallels to the Gospels (1951), p. 159. Morton
Smith concludes his excellent treatment thus: "I think these
passages suffice to show that Jesus appears in the Gospels in
a number of places where the parallel passages of the Talmudic
Literature have God or the Law. So much is fact. A likely inference would be that Jesus occupied in the minds of the authors
of the Gospels much the same place as God and the Law occupied
in the minds of the authors of the Talmudic Literature. But to
make such an inference would involve an act of historical
faith...." It would seem to us that the New Testament demands
that we make such an act.

[10]Cf. 1 John 2⁷ff.

support of such an interpretation of the words of Jesus the
Messiah, both Paul and John, like Matthew, could probably have
appealed to the tradition of the Messianic expectation of Judaism: the evidence for this given above may not be altogether
convincing but at least it makes such an interpretation not
wholly incompatible with Judaism.

But another factor emerges. Although Paul regards the
words of Jesus as the basis of a kind of Christian halakah, it
is Christ Himself in His person, not only or chiefly in His
words, who constitutes the New Torah: and so too in the Fourth
Gospel the New Torah is not only epitomized in the commandment
of agapê which finds its norm in the love of Christ for His own
and in the love of God for Christ, but is realized also in the
Person of Jesus, who is the Way, the Truth and the Life, i.e.,
the personalized Torah who is set over against Moses. This per-
sonification of Torah in Christ goes beyond anything which we
have found in the Jewish sources: there is there no premonition
of a Messiah becoming in Himself the Torah. Unless we follow
those Scandinavian scholars who find the king in the Old Testament, and therefore a fortiori, The Messiah, to be Himself the
source of Torah, or Volz, who found in Jeremiah 31^{31f} the expectation of a new type of human being in whose heart is the
well of obedience, - and these views are both unlikely - then
we must assert that those in the Early Church who saw their
Torah in Jesus Himself, as well as in His words, found not only
that any possible expectations of a New Torah that Judaism may

have cherished were fulfilled in Him, but that they were also transcended.[11]

---

[11]We suggest that it is possible that we are best to find the kind of seeds from which grew the personalization of Torah in Christ in such passages as those which speak of Wisdom (Torah) entering into men and making them friends of God (Wisdom of Solomon, 7^{14}, 27^{f}), or again in the idea of the nomos empsychos in Philo, See E. R. Goodenough, By Light, Light (1935), pp. 88, 196, etc. It is noteworthy that E. R. Goodenough connected Is. 42^{1-4} with the idea of the nomos empsychos, J. B. L., Vol. XLVIII (1929), p. 203, n. Kingship in early Israel.

INDEX OF AUTHORS

OLD TESTAMENT

Genesis
49:11   76

Exodus
12:17   57
32:31ff   10

Leviticus
13:3   59ff, 70
16:34   56, 57
23:21   57
23:41   57
27:34   88

Numbers
19:2   68f
24:17   46

Deuteronomy
1:37   10

3:26   10
4:6   42
4:21   10
6:7   22
9:17-20   10
9:25-29   10
10:16   19
11:19   22
17:18   61
17:19   21
18:15   10, 44, 90
30:6   19
30:11f   87
30:14   22, 87

Joshua
1:8   21

II Kings
14:6   24
17:26-27   32

Ezra
2:63   45

Esther
9:28   56

Psalms
1:2   21
2:7   90
31:1   77
37:31   21, 22
40:8   21
75:3   69
110:1   90
146:7   57f, 66

Proverbs
9:2   56
28:7   25

Ecclesiastes
2:1   71ff
12:1   71ff

Song of Songs
2:13   75
5:10   73

Isaiah
2:1   36
2:1-5   34
2:3   37
11:10   77
12:3   70, 71
26   73
32:6   70

42:1-4   31, 33, 34,
   38, 94
42:13   8
42:16   69
42:13-44:23   8
43:18-21   8
49:1-13   34
49:2   34
49:5-6   9
49:8-12   9
50:4-5   34
50:10   34
51:4   59
52:13   34
53:12   34

Jeremiah
4:4   19
5:4   32
7:7ff   18
16:14-15   8
26:4   24
26:18   37
31:31f   7, 13-28,
   90, 93
31:33   22, 23, 25
33:11   55
44:10   25

Ezekiel
11:9   23
36:26   23
36:27   23
38:16   36

Hosea
2:14-15   8
2:25   90

Micah
3:9-12   37
4:1-5   34, 37

Zechariah
11:12   77
13:2   68
14:6   69

NEW TESTAMENT

Matthew
5:17-20 4
5:18 52, 79, 83

Mark
1:27 71
7:14 88

John
1:21 44
1:25 44
6:14 44
7:40 44
13:34 92
14:15 92

Acts
3:22 44

Romans
7:1 83
10:4 83
10:6f 87

I Corinthians
2:9 82

II Corinthians
5:17b 8

Galatians
2:6 92

I John
2:7ff 92

Revelation
21:5 8

APOCRYPHA AND PSEUDEPIGRAPHA

2 Baruch
2:35 48
3:29ff 87

44:14 43

Damascus Fragment
1:7 46
8:2 47
8:5 47
8:6-10 46
8:8 47
8:9 47
8:10 46
9:8 46
9:10B 47
9:28B 47
9:29B 46
9:39B 46
9:53 46
15:4 47

Ecclesiasticus
24:3ff 42

1 Enoch
5:8 43
38:2 42
39:6 42
42:1ff 43
46:2 42
48:1 41, 43
49:1 41, 43
51:3 41
53:6 42
91:10 43

1 Maccabees
4:46 44
14:41 44

Psalms of Solomon
17:29ff 43

Testament of the Twelve Patriarchs
T. Judah 24:1 46
T. Levi 18:3 46

Wisdom of Solomon
7:14 94
7:27f 94

RABBINIC SOURCES

TARGUM

OTHER SOURCES

www.ingramcontent.com/pod-product-compliance
Lightning Source LLC
Chambersburg PA
CBHW020919090426
42736CB00008B/699